Teaching Math Through Storytelling

How to Design Engaging Lessons for the Elementary Classroom

**Gigi Carunungan
with Jessica Liou**

Teachers College Press
Teachers College, Columbia University

For
Ellis and Eli,
Hattie and Louie,
Risa and Nova,
and all the 21st century children
who continue to teach us
how children best learn mathematics

Published by Teachers College Press,® 1234 Amsterdam Avenue, New York, NY 10027

Copyright © 2025 by Teachers College, Columbia University

Cover design by Holly Grundon / BHG Graphics. Illustration by coauthor Jessica Liou.

Illustrations by Jessica Liou

Library of Congress Cataloging-in-Publication Data is available at loc.gov

ISBN 978-0-8077-8710-6 (paper)
ISBN 978-0-8077-8711-3 (hardcover)
ISBN 978-0-8077-8309-2 (ebook)

Printed on acid-free paper
Manufactured in the United States of America

Contents

Acknowledgments

This book draws inspiration from the dedication of teachers who innovate education for student success.

Educators in Guatemala, led by Patricia Barneond, Trae Holland, and Elizabeth Franke, sparked the concept and backed the design research to transform math learning.

Educators in the Bay Area, led by Dr. Angela R. Guzmán, Rebecca Lunceford, and Marisa Lerma, who facilitated in-class sessions featuring intercultural math stories for primary school students.

Ginger Leopoldo and Angela Agustin, after-school program instructors in Chicago, along with Vida Amanat, the after-school program coordinator of The Primary School in East Palo Alto.

Dr. Trena Wilkerson, past president and a member of the NCTM (National Council of Teachers of Mathematics) Board of Directors, along with curriculum and instruction experts. Dr. Eula Ewing Monroe and Laura Joy, who provided valuable insights on the intersection of math and literature.

Professor Tracey Tokuhama-Espinosa, whose belief in the vision of Math-Xplorers created the opportunity to bring this book to life.

Dr. David Whitenack, who provided the opportunity to teach the Math Methods Course at San Jose State University.

The Dissertation Committee, Chaired by Dr. Robert Gliner and members Dr. Noni Reis and Dr. Susan Charles, who guided the design study and a video documentary on teaching math with stories.

All the parents and primary school children who participated in the study from whom we learned how math stories enhanced and deepened their understanding of mathematics.

Jessica's parents, Lina and Peter Liou.

David Berkowitz, my spouse and calculus tutor, who has been a constant support.

Prologue
Why Math Stories?

> The child's world has the unity and completeness of his own life. He goes to school, and various studies divide and fractionize the world for him. . . . Facts are torn away from their original place in experience and rearranged concerning some general principles. Classification (of subjects) is not a matter of the child's experience.
>
> —John Dewey (1902)

This book aims to demonstrate how to help students achieve a state of flow and the ability to transfer in math learning by leveraging children's innate curiosity, creativity, and evolutionary mathematical abilities through meaningful, transformative, and enjoyable math stories and activities.

We explore the immersive and captivating medium of intercultural math stories with accompanying math learning games and activities. These stories provide children with practical reasons for learning mathematics. Children cultivate mathematical thinking as they tap into their imagination and logic to make sense of situations and problem-solve. Math stories inspire children to engage with teachers, peers, and family when learning to make mathematical sense and problem-solve.

THE IMPETUS TO ENRICH AND REINVENT THE WAY WE TEACH MATH

Early encounters with math profoundly shape a child's future. In an increasingly math-centric world, difficulties or fears formed in the primary grades hinder opportunities for 21st-century careers and social advancement.

Math education mainly assesses for understanding through quizzes at the end of a topic or chapter, quarterly tests, and standardized assessments. In an article in *The Atlantic*, Lahey (2014) explains that frequent testing supports remembering information. On the other hand, Weldon (2023) underscores how learning as test preparation drives anxiety and limits one's understanding of how mathematics influences and enhances life and work. As grades are mainly determined from test results, it makes sense that children perceive math learning as test preparatory activities. Scoring *high* on every type of assessment is the goal of learning mathematics. Every child's future lies in their ability to pass or fail these tests.

MOST CHILDREN FEEL ALIENATED, AND SOME ARE NOT CHALLENGED, IN MATH CLASSES

Our mission to generate a child-centric pedagogy or way of learning stems from experiences teaching and learning with children and adults. Designs of the math stories, games, and creative activities are inspired by neuroscience and validated by math teaching and learning practices. The humanist–constructivist philosophy, insights from the learning sciences, and the power and science of storytelling enlighten our understanding of how children connect to and learn mathematics. Experiences in formal and informal education environments affirm how mathematical understanding is underplayed when limited to memorizing facts and equation algorithms. Extending math to include illustrations and manipulatives creates more engagement. However, students wait for the teacher's next instruction after the activity. Children's curiosity drives the leap to agency in math learning, which fuels a sense of ownership over their learning journey. Curiosity inspires exploration and engagement, enabling children to drive learning and enter a *flow* state—immersed, focused, and deeply connected to the learning process. Flow builds the confidence and independence necessary to achieve agency in math learning.

Moreover, Luttenberger et al. (2018) highlight how assessments reflect the ways learners experience math anxiety and are challenged to achieve grade-level proficiency. For many students who struggle to engage with math, the subject can feel like deciphering an alien language, detached from their everyday experiences. The daunting task of memorizing abstract procedures, solving for precise answers, and recalling numerous formulas and facts often renders math inaccessible and dry.

Mathematics (math) anxiety describes the feelings of fear and apprehension that many individuals encounter when engaging with math (Ashcraft, 2002). Math anxiety arises from the pressure to recall every step and detail of calculation procedures coupled with the fear of making errors and experiencing more failures (Furner & Berman, 2003). In conversations with adults, they recount how lingering insecurities from past math classes resurface when tackling numerical calculations or discussing math-related topics. For many, the emotional impact of early math learning experiences persists, leaving lasting impressions through adulthood.

Correct Answer = Math Smart
Incorrect Answer = Math Failure

Kogelman and Warren (1979) explain how the prevailing notion that success in mathematics relies primarily on rote memorization of abstract content and following prescribed procedures perpetuates harmful myths about learning mathematics. The emphasis on solving for the correct answer and memorizing math facts leads to a lifelong fear of making mistakes and deeming oneself incapable of engaging with numbers and equations.

These false narratives, supported by grueling learning experiences, suggest that proficiency in math is an inherent trait reserved for *smart* individuals who are *good memorizers* and *abstract thinkers*, with *numbers brains*, further fueling feelings of inadequacy and discouraging interest in learning the subject of numbers and calculations for the rest of the population (Chestnut, 2018).

MULTICULTURAL AND INTERCULTURAL

Math stories are fiction narratives fueled by mathematical concepts. The stories exemplified in this book showcase multicultural characters reflective of today's learning communities. The characters encounter and explore mathematical ideas woven into the storyline, setting, imagery, and dilemmas.

Amyel likes to draw and build things.

Bikoy likes to write math equations.

Iliana likes to sing and dance.

Misha likes to ask "What if?"

Through their natural empathy for the characters, young readers are invited to participate in problem-solving. Our experiences and the recent study we conducted validate how children want to help the story characters. Narratives and questions ignite children's curiosity and inspire them to learn mathematical thinking strategies to make sense of situations and problems. Figuring out solutions for ill-defined and open-ended dilemmas requires creative thinking. Children merge their background knowledge with new ideas and model problem-solving solutions. With their responses woven into the narrative, readers role-play as young mathematicians and participate in the mathematical journey of the narratives.

The math stories explore math ideas and processes through intercultural narratives. Social and mathematical interactions among the multicultural characters reflect today's culturally diverse classroom populations. Engaging with peers from different cultural backgrounds and perspectives shapes the intercultural dynamics among students.

The efficacy of these books was tested with teachers and students in kindergarten and 1st grades in San Francisco Bay Area schools and after-school programs in Chicago and Guatemala. Utilizing design research, these exploratory studies highlighted how literary elements in fiction stories illuminated mathematical ideas. We observed children engaging in mathematical thinking as they connected with relatable multicultural protagonists and explored solutions to open-ended dilemmas woven in simulation-based scenarios.

While reading the page on the left, a student on the right instinctively counted the buttons on his shirt.

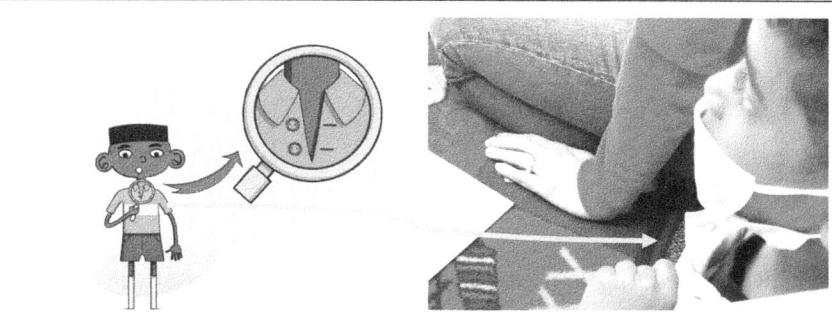

WHY MATH STORIES?

Math stories offer a nuanced approach to teaching mathematics to children. They bridge what is concrete and familiar in everyday life to mathematical ideas and processes, resulting in a meaningful understanding and appreciation of mathematics. The stories captivate children's curiosity, drawing them into imaginative and relatable narratives where they become active participants in the unfolding events.

In contrast, Klein (2022) notes that traditional math classes often leave students disengaged and restless when learning experiences are limited to solving equations and completing problems on worksheets without meaningful context. Children connect to math by integrating interdisciplinary elements that simulate real-world objects and places, utilizing real-world manipulatives related to the story. These story elements spark curiosity and empathy and drive children's perseverance in solving challenges.

Dialogue among the characters merge math equations and ideas. The characters' predicaments are designed as opportunities for sensemaking and problem-solving. Children empathize and are motivated to learn because math ideas are applied in context. Stirred by the stories, children engage with their responses, conversations, and experimentations.

The stories created are mindful of children's developmental traits, abilities, and potential. Learners are protagonists in their mathematical learning journeys. The stories' literary and mathematical elements provide diverse entry points for children to distill and apply mathematical ideas and processes.

Literary elements in math stories make mathematical concepts and procedures meaningful and relevant. Unlike traditional math methodologies that emphasize the pursuit of a single correct answer or a list of problems and equations to solve, math stories present combinations of unstructured, guided, and open-ended challenges with natural language, differently from the predetermined nature of structured math problems. Jimenez and Versachaffel (2014) elucidate how lessons in traditional math education are designed so that every math word problem must have a standard procedure for calculating the numbers presented. In math stories, problem-solving is a mystery or dilemma to be unraveled, tapping into children's innate sense of wonder, which inspires thinking of possibilities and experimenting in modeling solutions.

Captivated by the characters and images, learners eagerly follow the narrative, curious about what will unfold next. Children draw upon the mathematical concepts and procedures from the dialogues and descriptions of math ideas to model their solutions and explanations. Likened to a mystery, it feels like a puzzle to solve, and the clues are found in the narrative, character dialogues, and images. Math is not just an equation or a problem to be solved; the ideas and processes are integral in forming and moving the narrative. Math stories nurture and weave curiosity, logic, and creativity.

THE TEACHER-RESEARCHER-DESIGNER

Teachers are at the forefront of mathematics teaching and learning. Acknowledging their role in teaching and evaluating the effectiveness of pedagogical theories and curricular applications is essential. Higher education experts and learning designers typically act as researchers and authors of textbooks and curricula. The math education system tends to be highly centralized in choosing textbooks and programs. Primary school teachers comply and avoid conflict. Likewise, parents, older family members, and mentors in after-school tutoring and programs are generally expected to teach the prescribed curriculum, bundled with math practice problems and assessments. Mainly, teachers are instructed to teach with textbooks, with minimal opportunities to give feedback on students' responses to the topics and lessons.

Increasingly, studies on mathematics teaching and learning suggest that the quality of instruction is crucial for achieving lasting positive outcomes. There is, however, a wide range of definitions regarding what constitutes *quality* in teaching. Instructional strategies span hands-on learning, interactions between teachers and students as well as among peers, direct instruction, problem-based and inquiry-based learning, visual expressions, the use of music and movement, increased homework, parent and family engagement in math, one-on-one sessions, extended time for learning, deep dives, additional math sessions, and more. The Teaching and Learning International Survey (TALIS)—the largest international survey about teachers and school leaders—highlights that educators are just beginning to grasp what contributes to quality teaching (OECD, 2020).

In traditional math curricula, seatwork, homework, quizzes, tests, and assessments of students' performances determine their progress. However, these same tools also lead to anxiety about math among students. Instead of advancing, many students feel alienated by these textbook-driven practices. For decades, in what has been commonly referred to as the math wars, mathematicians, math educators, preschool and elementary school teachers, politicians, business leaders, STEM (science, technology, engineering, and math) specialists, and parents have been at odds regarding the universal criteria for quality math education (Smith, 2023). The absence of consensus among stakeholders highlights the challenge of defining and achieving quality math education. Teachers and children are caught up in conflicting perspectives. Developing teachers' agency by listening to their feedback is necessary for reinventing math learning. The National Council of Teachers of Mathematics (NCTM) Professional Learning Toolkit (2015) explains how *effective teaching practices support cultivating a positive identity and agency for teachers*.

In the next chapter, we will examine a child-centered learning framework by exploring research-based criteria that provide teachers with tools to observe, analyze, and identify what is effective for their students. Teachers are encouraged to build on children's innate ways of learning. By utilizing a framework that respects the nature of children, teachers can assume the role of researchers, enhancing their interactions with students to determine the efficacy of the curricula. In addition, teachers also take on the role of lesson designer as they revise, add to, and create activities to inspire students to engage, achieve flow, and transfer.

Math stories are informed by cognitive science, particularly research on how the human mind operates and learns most effectively. Li (2024), the founding director of Stanford University's Human-Centered AI Institute, shares her insights from experimental studies on the natural ways people think about various concepts. When someone observes an object, it quickly becomes linked to a place, an emotion, a context, and more. This observation swiftly shifts to interpretation, almost instantaneously influenced by a person's prior experiences and knowledge. Li's findings suggest that learning math, when presented as discrete and abstract topics, feels unnatural and can be arduous, as many have experienced in math class. Instead, associating an object with a space, situation, and other connections fosters personal meaning. The subconscious and immediate tendency toward association explains why children in our studies could master math concepts they had struggled with for one semester in just one story. Teaching by linking abstract math ideas with picture book stories that involve the senses, emotions, empathy, and relatable settings and challenges enhances the learning experience compellingly. ***Observe how this illustration from a math story utilizes association to describe math ideas. What do you notice?***

"What if I have **2** green buttons on one side and **3** pink ones on the other side?" asks Ramon.

"They are not **equal**," replies Maya.
Bikoy nods and draws a slash through the **=**.

"**2** is not equal to **3**."

AN INVITATION TO EMBARK ON A PERSONALIZED READING ADVENTURE

This book's writing style is grounded in socially oriented and interactive pedagogy, upholding the principles championed by constructivism and the learning sciences. We created activities for the readers to contribute insights, thus personalizing the theories and strategies presented. Here, the reader won't simply read. An element of this book called *Experiences* actively engages readers as protagonists of the book's narrative through activities highlighting personalized viewpoints.

Experiences engage readers in exploring simulations of mathematical concepts, applications, and learning strategies designed as hands-on activities and questions. Readers articulate key ideas through meaningful actions, reflections, insights, and opinions. Their involvement enhances authenticity and enriches the understanding of why and how math stories can elevate engagement and offer better opportunities for all students to achieve proficiency in mathematical knowledge and practice.

The Language of Math and Everyday Language

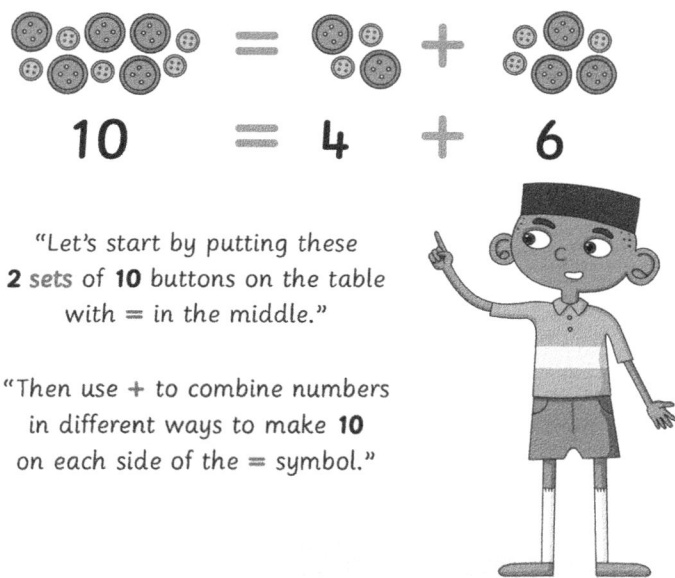

$$10 = 4 + 6$$

"Let's start by putting these **2 sets** of **10** buttons on the table with = in the middle."

"Then use + to combine numbers in different ways to make **10** on each side of the = symbol."

Mathematics is a quantitative discipline investigating the relationships between numbers, shapes, patterns, and structures. Concepts are typically expressed symbolically and explained through reasoning and analysis. Mathematical operations involve relating and manipulating numbers and symbols and observing patterns to solve problems.

Abstract thinking is intrinsic to mathematics. For example, math word problems differ from math stories, as the former lack narrative elements. Math stories integrate everyday natural languages with math vocabulary, embedding mathematical ideas and problems within familiar or novel contexts, characters, and narratives. While math problems state the problem, math stories tell a story. Picture book stories bridge the gap between the abstract nature of mathematical symbols and children's everyday languages and visual associations.

CHILDREN AS MATH LEARNERS

The complexities of children as learners are highlighted by the interdisciplinary nature and multifaceted framework for understanding used by the integrative field of the learning sciences. Young children arrive at school with layers of emotions and thoughts intertwined within human neural networks, actively making connections and meaning, whether conscious or not. Driven by experts in artificial intelligence, neuroscience, and other cognitive sciences, these disciplines are shaping a pedagogy that inherently and culturally connects with children and individuals from diverse backgrounds, abilities, qualities, and interests.

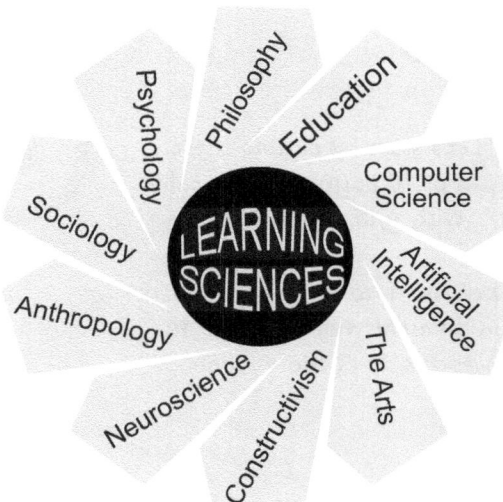

Additionally, the *science of stories*, also known as narrative psychology or narratology, provides an insightful lens for exploring the psychological and intellectual processes underlying storytelling and its impact on young people's behaviors, cognitions, and emotions. Peterson (2017) explains that when listening to a good story—rich in detail, full of metaphor, expressive of character—*we tend to imagine ourselves in the same situation.* Children enjoy role-playing like they were characters in their favorite stories.

The math stories are calibrated with developmental applications inspired by *constructivist* mathematicians, psychologists, and learning scientists and validated by real interactions with children. Through an interdisciplinary synthesis, these math stories are driven by multicultural characters creating intercultural interactions. Based on the phenomenal results of our studies, the math stories have emerged as a formidable learning solution for cultivating mathematical literacy and fostering children's love for math learning.

TRANSFORMATIVE PEDAGOGY

Flow and the Zone of Proximal Development

Agency refers to the ability to influence one's thoughts, behaviors, and beliefs in one's potential for success. *Flow* embodies agency in action; it represents an inspired, productive, and independent state of learning, much like how mathematicians and other professionals fully engage in their learning pursuits. Csikszentmihalyi (1975) introduced this concept in his book *Beyond Boredom and Anxiety*. The theory argues that learners achieve optimal outcomes when they tackle tasks that align their existing knowledge and skills with the challenges they encounter. An optimal learning state is characterized by the individual's interest in the task, a sense of control over the activity, and deep, focused concentration.

Vygotsky (1978), a cognitive psychologist, asserts that significant learning in children occurs through social interaction with a knowledgeable mentor. This tutor can demonstrate behaviors or provide verbal guidance to the child. A tutor can adopt various roles and solutions. In technology, a software program's algorithm directs users' interactions with a system. In a sense, it functions like a tutor for its users. Math stories are akin to a mathematics learning facilitator as they provide context, characters, journeys, emotions, and ideas.

Transfer is the holy grail of mathematics education. Children who learn math concepts in isolation often struggle without associative elements and a relational perspective among mathematical ideas and processes. Their inability to comprehend can stem from a lack of context, the abstract nature of symbols, and limited conceptual and relational comprehension. As a result, children find it challenging to apply their knowledge of mathematical ideas or algorithms to new situations, both within and outside of math classes. Moreover, students who only memorize facts have a weak foundation for tackling problem-solving tasks (Bransford & Stein, 1993). The ability to transfer knowledge is essential for students to achieve mathematical proficiency. *Proficiency* is defined as applying abstract mathematical concepts across various contexts and scenarios.

Unlike standard assessments, the framework and methodology rooted in mathematical proficiency and 21st-century applications differ from those of conventional math education. Mathematical proficiency and assessment benchmarks used in the math stories mentioned in this publication align with or are above the NCTM's grade-level proficiency expectations. Children who develop a sense of agency own their math learning and will relentlessly seek and create opportunities to learn more. Our studies showcase how math stories engaged children in the following:

1. **Conceptual understanding:** Grasping mathematical concepts, operations, and relationships
2. **Procedural fluency:** Carrying out mathematical procedures accurately, efficiently, and flexibly
3. **Strategic competence:** Formulating, representing, and solving mathematical problems
4. **Adaptive reasoning:** Using logic to explain and justify solutions
5. **Productive disposition:** Viewing mathematics as sensible, valuable, and worthwhile while believing in one's ability to succeed

Internal Drivers of Learning

We chose four crucial pedagogical ingredients that drive flow, transfer, agency, and proficiency: *necessity, curiosity, creativity,* and *community.*

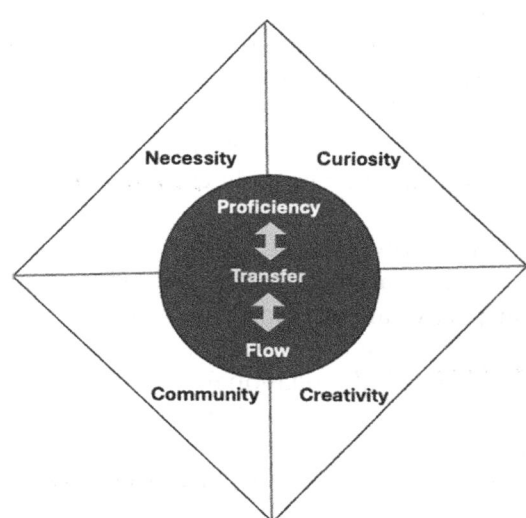

1. **Necessity** is the need to accomplish something. Empathy for the math story characters, background knowledge, logic, and social interactions contribute to the need to participate and figure out solutions.
2. **Curiosity** is a natural desire to explore, question, and understand. Unfortunately, fostering curiosity in young children is often neglected, as educational systems prioritize compliance towards a single solution over exploration with unknowns and varied results. Research indicates curiosity is closely associated with higher academic achievement—the internal drive to know and figure out.
3. **Creativity** is the ability to generate, explore, and express original ideas, solutions, or artistic expressions uniquely and meaningfully. It involves thinking beyond conventional boundaries, connecting concepts, and approaching problems with innovation and flexibility. Creativity builds upon other cognitive skills and integrates knowledge, comprehension, application, analysis, and evaluation to form unique outcomes. In a revised version of Bloom's Taxonomy by Anderson and Krathwohl (2001), creativity is placed at the highest level of cognitive processes.
4. **Community** is a supportive environment where children feel valued and included, encouraging collaboration and support among peers and teachers. Being part of a community offers children opportunities to learn from one another and develop a strong sense of ownership over their learning journey.

These four elements promote engaging learning experiences that spark and sustain children's interest in math. This book's chapters demonstrate ways to nurture these internal motivators in mathematics stories.

THE BOOK AND THE WEBSITE

While this book provides examples for primary school students, the strategies are also relevant for older students and adults seeking to refresh their foundational math concepts. Many adults, including teachers we've collaborated with, have shared that they wish they learned math with math stories. Had such stories existed, they would have enjoyed math class more.

We invite you to explore https://www.mathxplorers.org/ and dive deeper into intercultural math stories. Join us in cultivating a community of educators, parents, artists, and writers committed to humanizing and making math learning accessible to all.

We want to hear about and, when possible, support your ideas. Share your experiences and insights on integrating math stories into educational, community, and home settings. Contribute to the ongoing innovation of child-centered and intercultural math pedagogy, and incorporate mathematical thinking into daily conversations to make sense of situations, predict outcomes, analyze information, and solve problems. Let's work together to infuse joy into children's journeys of learning mathematics and nurture their unique identities as mathematical thinkers through engaging and inspiring math adventures.

CHAPTER 1

The Child's Mathematical Lens

What do you do?
We write and publish picture books for children.
That's so awesome! I love picture books! What kind of stories do you write?
Math stories.

When we talk about our writing, the word "math" almost always changes the tone of our conversations. *I don't like math. I'm not into math.* These are the most common responses we receive. On rare occasions, someone will say, *I like math. In school, I was good at math.* The word *math* evokes positive and negative emotional memories of how well or poorly one performed in the subject in school.

EXPERIENCE

How Do You Feel About Math?

Which of these emoticons represent your experiences learning math?

 Reflect: *Math is everywhere* rings *accurate* as a statement, yet traditional teaching methods often leave many children disconnected from the subject. Tutoring and homework typically focus on completing assignments and raising test scores, neglecting to *inspire genuine excitement and fulfillment* in math learning.

MATH ANXIETY PLAGUES MANY CHILDREN AND ADULTS

Around 93% of American adults report experiencing some degree of math anxiety. Estimates suggest that about 17% of the U.S. population experiences severe math anxiety (Blazer, 2011).

Carey et al. (2018) describe math anxiety as feelings of hesitation and heightened physiological responses when individuals engage in mathematical tasks. This anxiety can arise during activities such as manipulating numbers, solving math problems, or facing evaluative math-related situations. In a survey of various instruments measuring math anxiety, Silke et al. (2018) found that most studies agree on three facets that trigger the condition: ***test***, ***classroom***, and ***numbers***.

Math anxiety affects people on different levels. Spielberger (1985) describes how, emotionally, individuals suffer from feelings of tension, apprehension, nervousness, and worry. Blazer expounds physiologically that the symptoms of math anxiety can manifest as an increased heart rate, sweaty palms, upset stomach, and vertigo. Research utilizing functional magnetic resonance imaging (fMRI) by neurocognitive scientists Lyons and Beilock (2012) indicates that individuals with higher levels of math anxiety show increased activity in brain regions linked to detecting visceral threats and experiencing pain (bilateral dorso-posterior insula) when anticipating a math task. Interestingly, this increased activity is not observed during the actual performance of math tasks, postulating that the anticipation of math, rather than math itself, is perceived as painful.

EXPERIENCE

Our Math Mind Maps

Learning experiences are like weather. They are external conditions that affect how we feel, think, observe, and act.

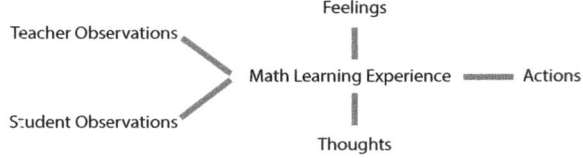

1. Take a moment to reflect on an unforgettable math learning experience.
2. Write the experience as a short phrase at the center of a blank sheet of paper.

3. Recall how the experience made you feel. Write the feeling(s) in a word or phrase above the experience.
4. Recall what you were thinking at that moment. Write the thought(s) in a word or phrase below the experience.
5. Recall your actions relating to the experience. Write these actions in short phrases to the right of the experience.
6. Recall what you observed of your teachers and classmates. Write these observations in short phrases to the left of the experience.
7. Connect the memories from steps 3–6 to the main experience with lines.
8. Continue to extend the mind map with other feelings, thoughts, actions, or observations.

Reflect:

- From your personal mind map, what can you infer about your math learning experience?
- How did the experience shape your ideas about learning mathematics?

Colleen Ganley, PhD, a developmental and educational psychologist, explains that you can make a mistake and get it wrong with math. *And that can be especially anxiety-provoking* (2019). Trezise and Reeve (2014) explain how emotions impact judgments and decision-making, and the divides between *people in math education and people who work in the psychology of math cognition* are barriers to overcome. Choe et al. (2019) conducted an experimental study on math anxiety, and the results confirmed their hypothesis that math anxiety is experienced by girls and boys as early as elementary school and can lead to avoidance of everyday situations using math later in their lives, including money management, career choices, and salary negotiation.

WHY SHOULD MATH MATTER TO CHILDREN?

According to the National Association for the Education of Young Children (NAEYC), a child's understanding of math at the start of kindergarten predicts future academic success more than early reading skills or attention abilities (Master, 2024). In today's educational landscape, math serves as an opportunity gatekeeper, influencing grade averages and limiting access to promising career prospects. As a core academic subject, a student's overall grade often depends on their performance in math assessments. Poor math performance affects academic standing and undermines confidence in one's abilities. Research shows that by fourth grade, many students start to develop fixed beliefs about their capabilities in subjects like math, which can impact their future learning and self-assurance. Positive early experiences can nurture a belief in one's ability to succeed in math, whereas negative experiences can result in feelings of inadequacy (Hwang, 2020). The requirements for college admissions typically include completion of high school math courses, particularly for majors in science, technology, and engineering, where proficiency in advanced math subjects is often expected. Falling short of these standards not only dampens enthusiasm for higher education but also limits opportunities for professional and social advancement. Research conveys people with high math anxiety are less likely to finish graduate school or pursue science, technology, engineering, or mathematics (STEM) careers (Weir, 2023).

CHILDREN THINK MATHEMATICALLY

Infants and toddlers are wired to want to know, and they figure things out when encouraged. In the following photos, a one-year-old is intently exploring the shape of a cup. She wonders how her hand can get into the cup. This is an intuitive math discovery activity. Children learn best when the pedagogy supports constructing their knowledge by building upon natural curiosity through discovery and exploration. Observe the child through her actions and how she knows when her hand adjusts to the shape of the cup.

The child's attention is captivated by the cup, sparking a sense of wonder.

The child circles the edge of the cup with her thumb.

The child folds her hand to the approximate size of the inner part of the cup.

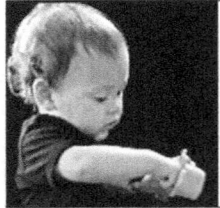
The child explores the cup with and in relation to her folded hand.

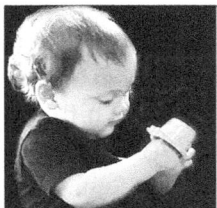 She discovers how her fingers fold into the interior and exterior parts of the cup.

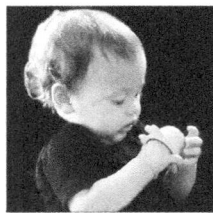 She observes the cup's smooth, solid, and unrelenting three-dimensional structure.

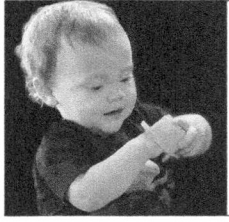 The child repeats the action of fitting her hand into the cup. She is delighted.

 A new discovery for the one-year-old child culminates with a sense of fulfilment.

Psychologist-educator Maria Montessori (1912) describes these actions as the *free, natural manifestations* of the *child*, further describing this moment of play with the cup as a *recognition of objects through feeling, that is, through the simultaneous help of the tactile and muscular senses.*

The cup, in this context, is a learning toy. The child's curiosity ignites the learning activity. Montessori (1912) expounds how this is a necessary phase of education because people learn about the world through the senses, in this case, tactile sense or touch and seeing. A child flexing her fingers in and around an object learns about flexible and rigid shapes through her touch sensory thinking channel.

Maria Montessori guiding a child in physically sensing geometrical insets.

The child in the activity demonstrates the actions of an integrated thinker. Unlike the more structured mathematics curricula in schools, this one is defined by the child's inner force: curiosity and the desire to explore multiple times until she is convinced that her interaction with the cup fulfills her goal. Observing the child's face allows us to infer her joy and focus on the activity. Children play to learn. Through the object, the child has created a lesson on three-dimensional objects, the interior and exterior elements of a cup, flexible versus rigid shapes, and more.

A toy at home sparked the lesson. This learning experience demonstrates the idea that math can be understood anywhere.

HUMANS ARE BORN WITH INNATE ABILITIES FOR MATHEMATICAL SENSEMAKING

Through evolution, infants are born with innate mathematical thinking abilities. They make sense of their surroundings, situations, events, objects, and occurrences in everyday life. Observe how toddlers interact with their toys; they arrange objects in various configurations. Young children differentiate between shapes, colors, sizes, and distances. They learn through sensory experience channels.

British math educator Richard Skemp (1976) advocates for a shift toward the relational math method, asserting that learning should cultivate students' sense of agency. Students develop a conceptual structure through this approach, enabling them to generate various plans or schemas limitlessly. Consequently, they approach math problems with a mindset oriented toward possibilities.

Contrastingly, Skemp criticizes mainstream math educators' use of *instrumental understanding*. This method requires students to grasp numerous fixed plans and meticulously follow each step, with the singular objective of reaching the correct answer to a problem. It involves following rules without reason. For example, we are taught to *borrow* in subtraction, with division, *turn fractions upside down*, and in multiplication, *negative times negative equals positive*. Skemp explains that the latter makes calculation and getting the answer quicker, simplifying one's understanding of mathematics by memorizing and mechanically solving problems with rules. Formulating problems in this way makes transferring the solution to contexts unclear when the issues are expressed differently. With discrete and rote learning, an essential concept of mathematics is missing: *Math rules are parts relating to a whole* (p. 9).

EXPERIENCE

Effects of Memorization

Question: What happens to children who naturally learn relationally when they are forced to memorize discrete math rules?

Steps:

1. Recall the rules you have had to memorize in math class.
2. List three rules.
3. Remember the positive and negative learning results by memorizing when the reasons supporting the steps are not explained.

Reflect:

- How would you teach these rules using a relational framework for understanding?
- How can creativity reinvent math learning into a child-driven lesson?

MATHEMATICS: AN EVOLUTIONARY ABILITY

Humankind's evolution has been intricately tied to our mathematical abilities, which are pivotal for human survival. Indeed, mathematics is not merely a subject but an essential aspect of our existence on Earth and in this world. Therefore, it is logical for humans to display an innate capacity for mathematical sense-making from infancy, a trait encoded in our genetic makeup. This inherent mathematical ability is evident even before formal schooling begins, as shown by the remarkable skills demonstrated by young children.

Infants and toddlers naturally engage in mathematical observation, effortlessly comparing attributes such as size, height, and quantity. They intuitively grasp concepts like big and small, tall and short, and more and less. Additionally, they develop an understanding of spatial relationships, discerning distances near and far. Moreover, children effortlessly integrate mathematical concepts into their daily routines, associating specific times with activities such as waking up, meals, and bedtime. They also develop a sense of duration, gauging the time it takes to travel to destinations long before they can read a clock.

Numerous studies demonstrate that children recognize small numbers in sets by age two as a natural process of making sense of their world. Coined by Kaufman et al. (1949) from the Latin word *subitis*, which means sudden, *subitizing* is the ability to quickly and accurately judge the number of items in a small group without counting them. Toddlers can differentiate between one, two, and three objects without counting. This is called *perceptual subitizing*. These innate mathematical abilities indicate the critical role of mathematics in human evolution, shaping our quantitative understanding of the world from the earliest stages of our development.

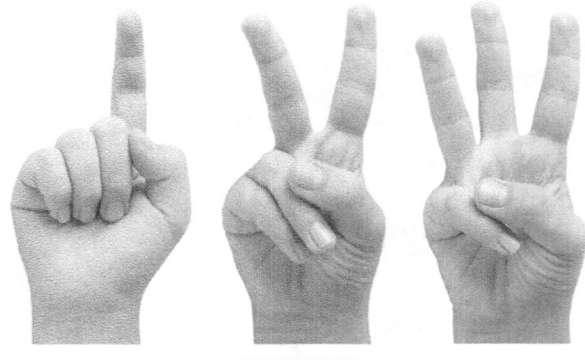

SUBITIZE
Instantly recognize one, two, and three objects without counting.

WHY IS MATH CHALLENGING FOR MANY?

Paradoxically, many children find themselves struggling to perform in math classes. For most adults, being "not a math person" stems from their encounters with math education, often characterized by memorization, rote learning, quizzes, tests, and standardized assessments. In his book, *The Child and Curriculum*, constructivist educator John Dewey (1902) argues that mainstream academic experiences designed by subject-matter experts for children are misaligned with the interests of children and how children think. This results in creating barriers to engagement and understanding. Meanwhile, math topics are organized according to abstract principles and presented discretely from their evolution and contexts.

*   *   *

While mathematical concepts stem from various circumstances, experiences, and the cumulative understanding of math principles, a disconnect occurs when they are taught discretely rather than relationally, and without considering the child's worldview and experiences (Dewey, 1902). Most parents and teachers instruct counting by having children recite and memorize. However, simply knowing how to enumerate numbers does not necessarily equate to understanding quantity. Without a solid number sense, early learners may struggle with discrete addition and subtraction tasks.

> *Failure to learn the conceptual basics of procedural knowledge and draw a relationship between this knowledge and the concepts leads to failure to build the models and decide where the procedures will be used. This manifests itself as a failure in problem-solving.* (Baykul, 2005)

When math learning focuses primarily on prescribed techniques and rote memorization, educators neglect to teach the essence of mathematics. As a result, overemphasizing procedural knowledge at the expense of conceptual understanding impedes children's understanding of math principles and their ability to model mathematically. This results in a decreasing sense of one's ability to learn math. Negative self-perceptions can hinder a student's ability to engage with and master mathematical concepts (García et al., 2016; Pekrun, 2011).

EXPERIENCE

Natural Math Abilities

Steps:

1. Assess the above ideas regarding children's natural math abilities through a small study.
2. How will you structure your research to assess children's natural math abilities?
3. Observe and document your observations based on children's actions and responses.

Reflect:

- What did you discover about young children and math learning?

FLOW AND THE ZONE OF PROXIMAL DEVELOPMENT

Csikszentmihalyi introduced the concept of flow in his book *Beyond Boredom and Anxiety* (1975). The theory suggests that learners achieve their best outcomes when they engage in tasks that acknowledge their backgrounds and skills while also presenting challenges. Such learning activities are characterized by the individual's interest in the task and a sense of control over the activity, resulting in deep, focused concentration. Flow-oriented activities offer optimal learning opportunities. Similar to deep-dive learning, these lessons equip students with the necessary tools and encourage them to utilize their unique backgrounds and abilities to explore and understand various situations. Children are motivated to find solutions despite their difficulties when they experience a state of flow. When designing lessons for flow, Jackson and Marsh (1996) explain that learners must manage their learning. However, Thanasoulas (2000) further elucidates that there needs to be a balance between autonomy and support. Recent studies and articles addressing school climate have highlighted a prevalent concern among educators: increased student misbehavior and declining interest in learning within K–12 classrooms. This phenomenon significantly indicates students' inability to connect, understand, and engage in class activities.

The overall environment and quality of life at school, often referred to as school climate, significantly impacts students' academic performance and behavior. A positive school climate fosters a sense of belonging, safety, and respect, which are crucial for students to thrive both academically and socially (Thapa et al., 2013). Therefore, ensuring that lessons are meaningful and connected to students' experiences enhances engagement (Newmann et al.,

1992). Think about how this can be achieved in classes with diverse students. Imagine a math class where students are in a state of *flow*.

MATH STORIES AND THE CHILD'S MATHEMATICAL LENS

When math is disconnected from context, students follow the teacher without understanding the mathematical ideas. With a limited background in mathematics, the discrete sets of facts and equations learned in class do not provide children with adequate conceptual recognition of these ideas and their relationships. Students struggle to transfer concepts to make mathematical sense of situations or solutions outside of how they were presented in class. With this observation and from studies analyzing students' performances in national and global math assessments, we explored placing mathematical concepts within engaging fictional stories to support students' sensemaking while also capturing their interest.

When we began our research, most students were hesitant, with some displaying disinterest and hostile behavior toward participating in our study. These students banged chairs, rolled on the floor, walked around the classroom, and more. Their teachers patiently reminded them about classroom rules and addressed their questions and complaints. The disruptive behaviors subsided. Then, the teacher began reading a math story and engaged them by asking questions. The students responded with empathy and curiosity.

The math stories we used were fictional narratives. When asked how they felt during the study, students responded that *the stories did not sound like math class*. Children are generally enamored by stories, with reading circles as one of their favorite learning activities. Our study used stories that introduced the children to a town called *Whatever*. The town's name was as far as possible from their usual concept of math as structured and serious. Furthermore, it was the first time children were invited to help people who thought they could not understand math.

In the town of Whatever, many people think they
cannot understand math. Is this possible? It truly is!
Would you like to do the math with people in this town?

This story is about Maya, a clothes maker,
and her friend Ramon, a button maker.

Maya sews colorful clothes with distinct designs.
Every shirt and pair of pants she makes is unique for each person.

This math story creates a context for mathematical concepts and incorporates cultural perspectives to make math personally relevant and understandable for students. A core message of the math stories is that everyone is unique. The goal is for each student to recognize their distinct backgrounds, personalities, gifts, and challenges. Classes consist of many individuals, making diversity a fact of life. While differences are celebrated, the stories demonstrate that mathematical thinking is universal. Finally, a critical component of utilizing math stories is creating learning activities that encourage a variety of student responses. Students' misconceptions that math is hard and that they aren't good at it are primarily fostered by previous math experiences where there's only one correct answer. You can help shift students away from these negative math misconceptions by designing lessons around open-ended problems.

SCAFFOLDING WITHIN THE STORY

Any math story plot should start by introducing foundational math ideas to familiarize students with the problem they will solve. The story starts out with a problem: *We need to help Ramon, the button maker, organize his buttons in a button box.* This is an opportunity to introduce and explore the concept of sets.

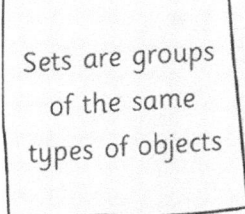 

Sets are groups of the same types of objects

During our study, Teacher Rebecca guided her students to explore the concept of sets beyond visual objects. She included hand claps, rhythms, sound volumes, and more. Students created sets based on their criteria for similar types of objects. Teacher Rebecca encouraged sensemaking by posing questions to enhance her students' observational skills. *What do you notice?*

I group the buttons with the same color, same size, and oh same buttonholes!

1 + 3 + 3 + 3 and my answer came up to 10.

Teacher Rebecca creates a class event where students share their sets with their peers. This forum, based on the children's work, allows the learners to reason mathematically based on their sets and learn from their peers.

AN OPEN-ENDED PROBLEM

"Oh gosh, I must have made a mistake, says Maya. Clothes need to have the same number of buttons and buttonholes."

Kilpatrick et al. (2001) discuss the role of open-ended problems in connecting mathematical concepts and enhancing understanding. Free from judgment as right or wrong, students tapped into their innate abilities, such as curiosity, creativity, and pattern recognition. They intersected newly learned math ideas with early math knowledge, which included sets, addition, and subtraction.

Given the initial success of building sets, students' enthusiasm to assist the characters in solving the tall man's missing buttons became palpable. They needed to elevate this math concept into a strategy for a solution. By doing so, students felt they were part of the story and were excited about the challenge of becoming young mathematicians. Through the narrative, students were eager to learn more math.

*Bikoy, Maya, and Ramon count **1**, **2**, **3**, **4**, **5** buttons!*
*Bikoy explains the **total** number of buttons is **5**.*
*In math, **total** is the word used to say **all**.*

Mathematical ideas enrich the narrative. As language skills grow, mathematical vocabulary integrates into everyday conversations, like the dialogue of the story characters.

On the second day of our study, the students were busy figuring out how to solve the problem, given that Ramon, the button maker, makes sets of no more than five buttons. The teacher observed her class, and every student was in a flow state. In just two lessons, students who had once been reticent to participate in math were actively enjoying the problem-solving process, persisting through challenges and coming to unique solutions.

Throughout this book, we'll explore how to cultivate a positive math mindset and create engaging math stories that resonate with students. We'll prepare you to teach your math stories, provide practical advice on facilitating the learning experience, and clarify how to assess student learning. By the end of this book, you will have become a math story writer and storyteller, and you'll feel confident that you can make math engaging for all your students.

CHAPTER 2

Deep-Dive Learning With Math Stories

EXPERIENCE

Compare Three Learning Experiences

Materials:

- 2–3 small bowls
- Tap water
- Ice cubes
- Thermometer

Steps:

First Experience

1. Bowl 1: Fill half a small bowl with tap water.
2. Wrap your hands around the bowl for five seconds. Feel the temperature with your palms.
3. Take an ice cube with kitchen tongs and drop it into the bowl with tap water.
4. Wrap your hands around the bowl for five seconds. Feel the temperature with your palms.
5. Record your observations.

Second Experience

1. Bowl 2: Fill half of a small bowl with tap water.
2. Grab a cube of ice with your hand.
3. Dip your hand and ice cube into the water bowl.
4. Keep your hand and ice in the water for five seconds.
5. Record your observations.

Third Experience

1. Use a thermometer to measure the water temperature in bowls 1 and 2.
2. Record your findings and observations about learning.

Reflect:

- How can the above experiences serve as analogies to different ways of learning math?
- Analyze the experience as it supports:
  - » Acquiring new knowledge and skills
  - » Curiosity
  - » Creativity
  - » Meaning
- How do these activities demonstrate deep-dive learning?

These analogies are meant to explore the impact of learning strategies. Specifically, *how we learn is what we know.* There are no right and wrong answers.

This chapter explores deep-dive learning and how math stories provide rich contexts, language, and structure to engage students in meaningful and authentic (as opposed to discrete and shallow) mathematical learning. Through these strategies, the goal is for children to thrive in mathematical thinking practices, raise their mathematical proficiency, build agency, and get excited about math learning.

The ideas in this chapter are organized into three parts:

1. Reframing Mindsets on Underperformance in Math
2. Creativity Through Exploration and Mathematizing
3. Deep Dive Learning With Math Stories

REFRAMING MINDSETS ON UNDERPERFORMANCE IN MATH

Our study on the effectiveness of math stories was conducted in partnership with school leaders and teachers in schools where 70–85% of the students were performing below expected math grade-level proficiency. The research also extended to students enrolled in after-school programs. The children represented a population diverse in abilities and cultural backgrounds.

Each time we began the study with a group of 5–7-year-olds, we noticed that the children were not enthusiastic about attending another math class. However, with all groups, the children's attitudes shifted when the teachers read the math stories. The narratives immediately captured their interest. Students empathized with the characters' dilemmas and were motivated to help solve their problems by participating in math games and problem-solving activities. The teachers were surprised by how their students mastered mathematical concepts and processes they had struggled with in one semester with one math story. Moreover, the children enthusiastically devised solutions that blended creativity with mathematical thinking.

Underestimating Math Abilities of Low-Income and Children of Color

Deficit thinking mistakenly attributes students' academic struggles to perceived shortcomings in their backgrounds, cultures, and family environments rather than addressing systemic issues or the quality of instruction they receive. Harvard professor Delpit (1988) critiques the excessive reliance on explicit instruction for minority students, contending that it can restrict their access to meaningful learning experiences. When systemic barriers are ignored, the blame for academic failure is unfairly placed on underperforming students and their families, reinforcing the judgment they only need basic instruction to advance to the next grade level (Carter & Welner, 2013; Kozol, 1991).

The current educational system, which frequently alienates and emotionally obstructs learning through demeaning and discouraging teaching methods, perpetuates harmful stereotypes accusing low-income and children of color of lacking the ability or motivation to succeed academically (Valencia, 2010). This pervasive typecasting suggests that these students are inherently less capable, leading to lower expectations from educators and policymakers (Garcia & Guerra, 2004).

Creative Mathematical Experiments

The traditional approach to mathematics education emphasizes teaching specific algorithms and procedures. Focusing on memorizing rules and steps disconnected from children's realities dissuades exploring different problem-solving methods. As a result, this approach fails to nurture creativity and overlooks the significance of attaining a deeper understanding of underlying concepts.

The primary goal of reinventing math learning was to address traditional teaching methods that have long alienated generations of students from mathematics. Our aim was to develop replicable and scalable approaches rooted in constructivism and insights from cognitive, social, and psychological sciences. From our teaching experiences, we have observed how much children enjoy listening to and reading stories. When merged with math ideas and practices, stories give purpose to math learning. Story elements make math ideas comprehensible.

The ultimate goal of our design research was to determine whether under-performers could elevate their understanding of math concepts beyond grade-level expectations and gain agency through the stories. Math stories provide language-rich applications of mathematics and create opportunities to achieve dual learning goals: reading and math. They offer various access points for all children with relatable narratives, characters, and simulations of real-world problems.

The design study was conducted with various groups of children in classroom settings, during after-school programs, and in family environments. Design research involved observing users in their natural environments and gaining insights on the challenges and breakthroughs of teaching math through stories.

Design research emphasizes understanding the processes and the users through which learning occurs. It tests whether and how a solution works. The study was conducted in educational settings to produce relevant and applicable findings. The design research method bridges the gap between theory and practice, allowing observations of how the math stories discussed in this book functioned in classrooms.

By observing students' interactions with math stories in their learning environments, we assessed how these stories contribute to a deeper understanding of math concepts. Moreover, the results offered insights we used to refine the stories, enhancing their effectiveness in helping students achieve conceptual understanding, flow, and transfer.

Reinventing Math Learning With Stories

Fiction intertwines with mathematical concepts. In the math story "Pipa the Architect," young children explore various methods for calculating the total area of a space. The characters in the story design floor plans using square-inch tiles as a unit of measurement. The narrative deliberately avoids introducing the algorithm *Length times Width* or *Area = L × W*. While the standard benchmarks do not expect kindergartners, 1st-, and 2nd-graders to know multiplication, they can discover different ways to compute area by utilizing their background knowledge and the story's clues.

"Let's group the tiles in each room into sets of 10.
Then count how many there are," says Iliana.
"I love counting by 10s!" sings Ruby.

"I love counting by **10**s!"
sings Ruby.

Here is an example of a child's floor plan and equation.

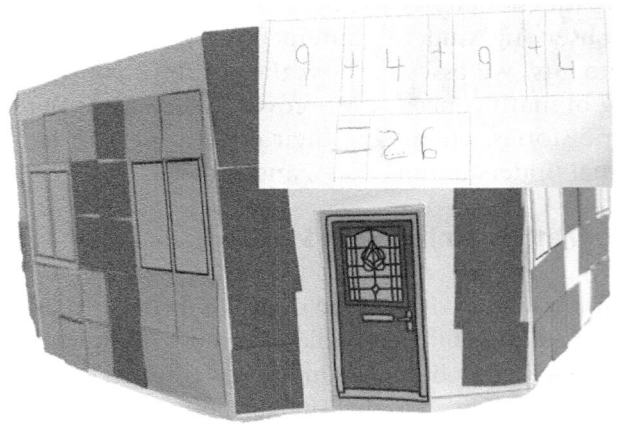

The study observed K–2 children calculating the *area* of their floorplans (most without using multiplication). Using unstructured and open-ended problems, we noted how the constraints on creativity in mathematics education are mainly due to a focus on procedural learning, standardized testing, and narrow perceptions of mathematics. A report by the NCTM highlights the negative impact of standardized testing, noting that it often narrows the curriculum and discourages innovative teaching practices (NCTM, 2014).

The study underscores why math learning should not focus primarily on passing tests. Professional mathematicians approach problems with curiosity and creativity, often exploring various methods and strategies to find solutions. They don't simply apply known formulas. Mathematicians question assumptions, observe patterns, test new procedures, and formulate theories from extensive explorations. Likewise, mathematical exploration is essential in fields utilizing math applications, such as engineering, economics, business, data science, politics, and the natural, medical, and social sciences. In these applications, math influences innovative solutions for complex challenges.

At its core, math is a discipline rooted in problem-solving, critical thinking, and exploring abstract ideas in symbolic mathematical language. It is used to shape understanding and real-world solutions.

CREATIVITY THROUGH EXPLORATION AND MATHEMATIZING

Scuba divers don't just plunge into oceans; they train and use tools to ensure their safety. Once they dive into the deep, they find themselves immersed in an unfamiliar and uncontrolled world. Curious and with their background knowledge, they use tools to explore unpredictable waters. Their training, instruments, and techniques enable them to make sense of and navigate the wild depths of the sea. Every experience is transformative. With challenges, successes, and discoveries, divers yearn to dive deeper and learn more. Similarly, deep-dive learning aims to engage students by encouraging them to explore, discover, invent, and experiment. Learning involves use of mathematical concepts, techniques, and tools to elevate comprehension and practice.

Deep-dive learning is an immersive process designed to develop a profound understanding of concepts, foster critical thinking, and encourage students to engage comprehensively with the material. The method involves various learning activities, such as exploration, analysis, experimentation, and reasoning, to cultivate math learning. *Through open-ended questions, children are encouraged to seek multiple solutions.*

Kant and Sarikaya (2020) underscore that there are no limits to inventing various ways to solve a problem mathematically. Open-ended questions encourage diverse ideas in the mathematizing process. Specifically, deep-dive problem-solving engages students to experiment with heuristic strategies, think critically, and develop creative solutions (Hmelo-Silver, 2004; Polya, 1945). The learning experience simulates how mathematicians engage in problem-solving. Exploring and discovering multiple ways and developing new strategies and insights is progress in the mathematical field.

Designed as unstructured problems, students learn by exploring strategies to approach and resolve dilemmas. Tackling unstructured problems with mathematical modeling involves identifying key elements within a context, nurturing children's *mathematizing* (Freudenthal, 1991; Polya, 1945). When math learning activities focus solely on finding the correct answer or restrict learning to practicing specific skills, various approaches to a problem are often overlooked.

Mathematizing

Dutch mathematician and educator Hans Freudenthal (1968) coined the term *mathematizing*, which refers to the *fundamental activity of doing mathematics or, more precisely, of introducing, using, varying, and applying mathematical symbolism.* He argues that math is not a closed system but an activity. Van den Heuvel-Panhuizen (2003) elucidates that Freudenthal's concept of mathematical education does not particularly emphasize mirroring reality but *as a process of mathematizing phenomena from the physical world and abstract structures.*

The concept of mathematizing—interpreting and expressing real-world situations through mathematical representations—is well-established in educational literature. A learner-mathematician acquires knowledge by experimenting with symbolic notation to represent mathematical content. Kant and Sarikaya (2020) elaborate further on the concept of mathematizing, explaining that Freudenthal emphasizes the importance of engaging children in this process. Freudenthal categorizes mathematizing into two levels. The first level is *horizontal mathematization*, which involves observing the real world and using mathematical tools to abstract and solve problems. For example, when you organize an unstructured collection of objects to count how many there are, you engage in horizontal mathematization. This process applies mathematical concepts to understand and address problems within our physical environment.

Antonio has a different idea: "Let's tally all the tiles on our floor plan,
then skip count by 5s to find the total!"
"How fun!" claps Manuel. "Can you teach me how to tally?"

Vertical mathematization is the second level of mathematizing. This involves analyzing the relational attributes of mathematical ideas expressed through symbols tested through operational combinations. Then, the teacher guides students in verifying the accuracy of the symbols applied to mathematical models and the structure of the model itself. By learning through exploration and leveling up, mathematizing encourages students to think critically and creatively, advancing their problem-solving skills (Hmelo-Silver, 2004).

Playing Is Learning

Play-based activities prepare children for in-depth exploration. Hedegaard et al. (2020) define play as a social context that influences children's investigation of objects and relationships. Play is a spontaneous and enjoyable activity that is usually self-directed. It allows individuals, especially children, to explore, experiment, and engage creatively and imaginatively with their environment. Play is often characterized by a sense of fun and freedom, where the rules are invented (as in games) and the primary focus is on the process rather than the outcome. Children naturally gravitate to playing, essential for cognitive, emotional, and social development. Play can take many forms, including physical activities, role-playing, games, and imaginative scenarios. Through play, individuals develop problem-solving skills, learn to interact with others, and gain a deeper understanding of the world around them. Play encourages children to be curious and adventurous and develop self-regulation.

We observed the level of the children's concentration during problem-solving. Most of the children exclaimed, *"It felt like we were playing!"* Through play, children explore and experiment, leading to student insights. Play helps students deepen their mathematical understanding without the pressure of simply finding the one correct answer. It encourages their enthusiasm and joy in discovering and applying creativity, which broadens their mathematical knowledge and skills. Laurel Bongiorno (n.d.) of the National Association for the Education of Young Children (NAEYC) explains that play nurtures positive attitudes and brings joy to children's learning, reducing anxiety and stress.

Increased Engagement, Motivation, and Agency

Math stories enthuse students with embedded math ideas and challenges in real-world contexts. Making math ideas tangible increases students' interest and motivation to learn. Deci and Ryan (2000) highlight the importance of how intrinsic motivation is enhanced when learning activities are exciting and relevant to students. Fueling the internal drive is crucial in mathematics learning because it motivates students to participate in the subject out of genuine interest and a desire to understand and solve problems. When motivated, students are more likely to persevere through challenges, explore concepts deeply, and develop a lasting appreciation for mathematics.

On the following story page, children are introduced to *square inches*, a unit of measurement used to measure *area*. This is an advanced concept for 5–7-year-olds. We observed that when children saw the value of the math idea as necessary for designing their floor plans, there was no limit to what they could learn.

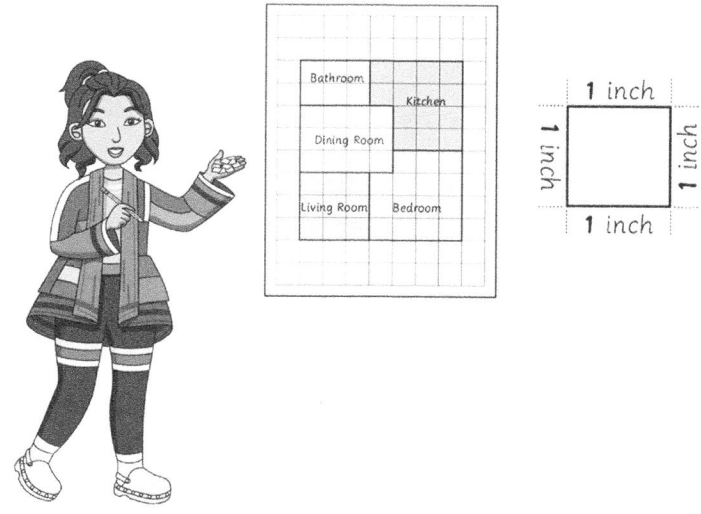

Pipa shows everyone her square-inch tiles.
"I use these to help make my floor plans,"
explains Pipa.
"Why do you think these are called
square inch tiles?"

Children Must Know the Reason for Learning Math

A key element of sustaining deep-dive learning is Lev Vygotsky's (1978) theory of the *zone of proximal development* (ZPD). This concept refers to the difference between what a learner can do independently and what they can achieve with guidance and collaboration. ZPD is a critical variable in the social process of teaching and learning. Children learn with teammates; they discuss, explore, and solve problems together. Deep-dive learning actively transforms learners into active participants, leading knowledge and skills acquisition, as they *interpret*, *articulate*, *model*, and *engage* in various forms of understanding and articulation.

Russian educational psychologist V.V. Davydov emphasizes the importance of developing agency through participation in learning. He defines a learning activity as human actions characterized by the logic of discovery. In this context, students should not merely comply. Rather, they should understand and agree to the activity's goals to fully engage. Agency involves students learning how to independently and authentically acquire knowledge. Davydov refers to this as the unity of mind and activity (Sidnev, 2020).

In the following image, the teacher creates circles to guide the organization of the objects.

Through literary, visual, and mathematical elements in a math story, the teacher or parent facilitates problem-solving and enhances understanding. Interactions with peers, teachers, and family bridge the gap between a child's ability, knowledge, and potential level. Learning in a supportive and empowering social environment, where children's ideas are appreciated, inspires and challenges learners to persevere and achieve a more profound understanding.

Long-Term Retention and Transfer

Working on meaningful, context-rich problems helps children build a firm grasp of mathematical ideas, making their understanding more relevant and lasting. Learners who *explore* math in real-world situations understand its importance and apply what they learn in different situations. This is *transfer*.

EXPERIENCE

Compare and Contrast

Materials:

- Worksheet on area equations
- Pencil
- Graphing paper
- Crayons

Activity:

First Experience: The Worksheet

1. Use a standard worksheet on area equations. Introduce students to the formula:

Area = Length × Width.

Teach by exemplifying how to solve for area.
2. Have students solve for the area on three equations in the worksheet. Assist as needed.

Second Experience: Imagine and Design a Floorplan

1. Show students a floor plan of your family house.
   Here is an example from the story "Pipa the Architect":

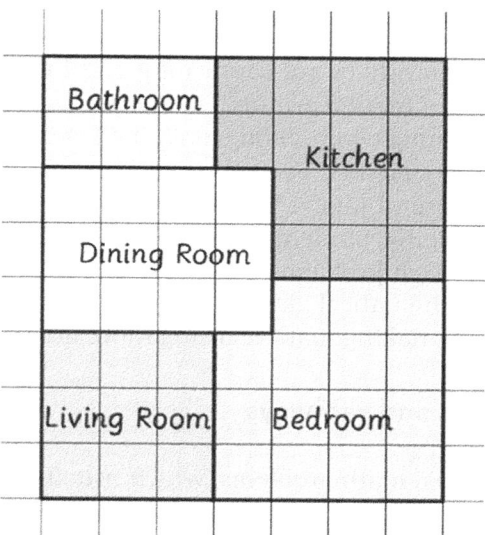

2. Group students into pairs. Each pair will create a floor plan for a family of two children and two parents. Provide multicolor square-inch tiles and 1-inch graphing paper for each pair.
3. Instruct the pairs to calculate the area of their floorplans.
4. Have students share their strategies for calculating area.

Reflect:

- How can these experiences serve as analogies to different ways of learning math?
- Analyze the experiences as they support:
  » Acquiring new knowledge and skills
  » Curiosity
  » Creativity
  » Meaning

DEEP DIVE LEARNING WITH MATH STORIES

Fictional stories are imagined realities, much like floor plans. In the previous activity, students designed and calculated the area, but they will need more inspiration to continue contemplating the math they learned after class. Creatively crafted scenarios connect to children's lives and background knowledge while engaging their imaginations. Stories are memorable and engage the logical, creative, and emotional aspects of their minds. The emotional component creates the most significant impact. The emotional connection fostered by stories is crucial in helping children understand themselves and others better. Narratives are captivating and inspire children to elevate their understanding of math learning. Fiction stories significantly enhance creativity in math learning by providing make-believe contexts that liberate students from the anxiety created by one-correct-answer word problems. Stories can embody a culture of taking risks and recognizing mistakes as a step forward in solving problems. Students not afraid of failing are likelier to explore new ideas and approach problems from different angles (Csikszentmihalyi, 1996). Integrating mathematical ideas and engaging narratives elevate mathematical understanding, making math learning more accessible and exciting.

Multiple Solutions and Pathways

Unlike traditional math problems, which usually have a single correct answer, fictional contexts allow for the exploration of diverse methods and solutions, fostering curiosity and creativity. Fiction is compared to an invitation to an open field of possibilities, where scenarios reveal numerous options, encouraging students to make sense of mathematics and think critically and divergently.

Structured Versus Unstructured Math Problems

Structured and unstructured math problems represent two distinct types of mathematical tasks used in educational settings to develop various skills and levels of understanding. *Structured* math problems are typically well-defined with clear, specific directions to solve for a single correct answer.

Characteristics
- **Explicit instructions:** These problems provide all the necessary information to solve them.
- **Single solution:** There is typically one correct answer or a set of steps that lead to the solution.
- **Procedural orientation:** Focuses on applying known procedures or formulas.

Example:

To find the area of a square or rectangle, multiply the length by the width. The total area will be the sum of the area of the rectangle and the squares. Find the total area of this shape:

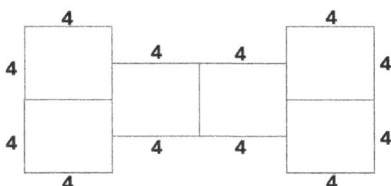

Unstructured or open-ended math problems are less defined and may have multiple paths to a solution and multiple correct answers. They are designed to engage students in mathematically interpreting real-world situations by modeling the problem and the solution.

Characteristics
- **Ambiguous conditions:** These problems might provide only some of the details required, requiring the solver to identify missing information.
- **Multiple approaches and solutions:** There can be various ways to approach and solve these problems.
- **Critical thinking and creativity:** They encourage exploration, hypothesis testing, and innovation in problem-solving.

Example:

"Next, we will need to count how many tiles were used for each house," Pipa guides the teams. "The total number of tiles is the area of the floor plan. This number tells us how big or small a house is."

EXPERIENCE

Structured Versus Unstructured

Steps:

1. Think of a structured problem.
2. Translate this into a story scenario with an unstructured problem.
3. Share these two versions in your class. Observe the students' responses relating to curiosity and creativity and what they learned mathematically.
4. Ask students to compare how they felt and what they learned when solving the problems.

Reflect:

- What were your observations of student learning?
- What insights about structured and unstructured problems did you get from this experience?

Emotional Engagement and Empathy

Working with fictional scenarios, characters, and challenges gives children greater freedom to think flexibly and creatively. Fictional stories broaden possibilities. For instance, a math lesson set in an imaginary world, where students apply geometry to design a castle or use algebra to break a magical spell, makes the math content more relatable and exciting, fostering a desire to participate and succeed.

While deep-dive learning in mathematics may initially seem daunting due to its complexity and divergence from traditional teaching methods, its benefits in student understanding, retention, and reduced anxiety are significant. It fosters a deeper, more engaging, and fulfilling learning experience, equipping students with the skills necessary to navigate the complex world of mathematics. Deep-dive learning reflects how mathematicians engage in their work. This practice encourages more insightful, adaptable, and capable young minds to think mathematically. Embedding mathematical concepts within imaginative stories helps children connect emotionally with the material, increasing enthusiasm, resilience, and retention. Math stories transform anxiety-ridden math learning by nurturing children's curiosity and encouraging the sharing of ideas in problem-solving without fear of failure. The relatability of the characters and situations creates a sense of empathy and fulfillment as readers help the characters by solving their challenging math problems.

Math stories can help students model complex problems and test and evaluate different solutions. Children's creative ideas expand their mathematical understanding. Cooperative learning with peers weaves multiple viewpoints, preparing them to succeed in future collaborative work environments.

Generalizing is key to conceptual mathematical understanding. It serves as a bridge connecting isolated facts and methods to broader concepts, facilitating more profound understanding and more versatile problem-solving skills. Math stories empower students to generate concepts using multiple access points, relatability, open-ended problems, and emotional links. Story elements make math ideas meaningful to children. Narratives facilitate the development of the ability to generalize in mathematics.

Review of Deep-Dive Learning

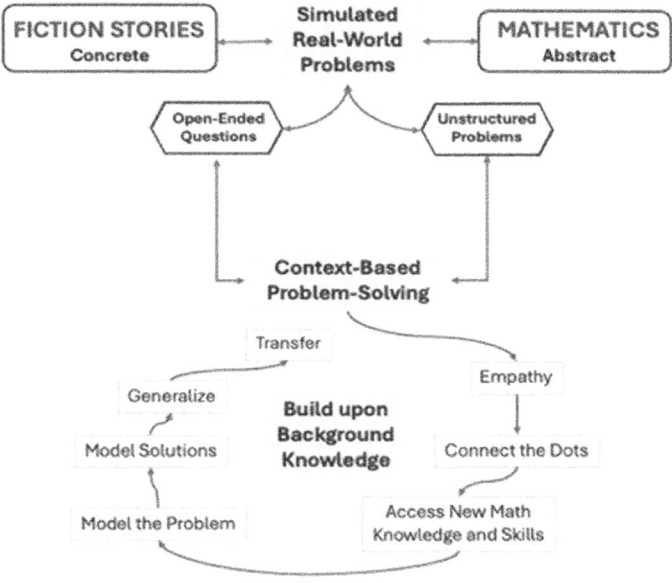

Math stories serve as pedagogy for deep-dive learning. Immersed in an imagined world, time, space, characters, and situation stir a child's sense of purpose—the *need* to learn math. This fuels curiosity and a desire to know more. Children's creativity flourishes as they combine their background knowledge with new insights, discovering multiple ways to mathematically solve the characters' problems so the narrative can progress. The learner is at the heart of the math learning experience, making sense of mathematics by modeling the problem, exploring solutions, and generalizing math concepts. Peer-to-peer interactions foster a dynamic and enthusiastic learning community. Engaging deeply with math stories, I quote the children in the study: *It feels like playing. Math is so much fun.*

EXPERIENCE

Review of Deep-Dive Learning

Steps:

1. Review the model on math stories and deep-dive learning.
2. How do the elements of the model highlight the insights you distilled from practicing with unstructured math problems?

Reflect:

- How can deep-dive learning be implemented in a traditional school schedule?
- How can math skills development be achieved with deep-dive learning?

CHAPTER 3

Learning Mathematics in the Intercultural Way

EXPERIENCE

The Intercultural Lens: Seeing and Thinking Differently

Materials:

- 3D object
- Chair
- Table

Steps:

1. Place a 3D object on a table.
2. Sit in a chair on one side of the table and look at the object. What do you see?
3. Sit in a chair on the other side of the table and look at the object. What do you see?
4. Sit on the floor. Look at the object. What do you see?
5. Stand on the chair. What do you see?

Reflect:

1. Try this in your classroom. Instruct students to form a circle and then close their eyes.
2. Position a three-dimensional object at the center of the circle. Have the students open their eyes, observe the object, and describe what they see. Each child shares their perspective—one object with multiple impressions.
3. Ask your students why they see things differently when seeing the same object.
4. Write a math problem on the board. For younger children, encourage the use of manipulatives to demonstrate the problem. Instruct students to share their views on the problem.

Reflect:

- What happens when you look at the object from multiple sides?
- How do differing views affect the way children learn math?

This activity demonstrates how a single object can generate multiple impressions. Similarly, in the context of learning, children's diverse cultural backgrounds and experiences lead to various responses to lesson strategies.

Mathematics as a discipline evolved through historical intercultural contexts thanks to the contributions of individuals and communities worldwide. Mathematical concepts are human constructs that developed from these intercultural contexts. For example, the number system is a product of global cultural intersections. Applications in various societal contexts fostered the growth of mathematical ideas. Mathematicians built upon and expanded mathematical concepts with new practices, technological applications, and inventions of theorems.

This chapter discusses math stories as an intercultural process grounded in the multicultural backgrounds of children, their families, and communities. Influenced by their sociocultural perspectives, children connect with the narratives, images, and challenges embedded in math stories in diverse ways. Through distinct cultural lenses, children shape their purpose and meaning of mathematics. The contexts in the stories illustrate how multicultural communities can live, work, and thrive by creating opportunities to explore, discover, and develop agency in mathematics.

MATHEMATICS IS THE MOST UNIVERSAL OF LANGUAGES YET THE MOST MISUNDERSTOOD OF SUBJECTS

Leap (1988) shared a story about a Ute student. To contextualize, more than half of the population of this Native American tribe resides in the Uintah and Ouray reservation, located in northeastern Utah.

> The Ute student was asked to determine how much his brother would have to spend on gasoline if he wanted to drive his truck from the reservation to Salt Lake City. The student responded: My brother does not have a pickup. (p. 176)

The student's response demonstrates how, as Rauff (1993) explains:

> Context, actuality, sociality, language, ways of learning, ways of knowing, and other culturally mediated components of mathematics and mathematics learning are significant factors in how people learn or don't learn mathematics. (p. 42)

MATH AND CULTURE

Schoenfeld (2002) critiques the cultural influences on pedagogy, pointing out that certain teaching practices prevent students of color from passing algebra, thereby impacting their high school graduation rates. He emphasizes that math is a universal language, enabling mathematicians from various linguistic backgrounds to share a common understanding of mathematical concepts. Schoenfeld illustrates this point with the following example:

> A square is a square is a square: once one states that a quadrilateral in the Euclidean plane is a square, then (for example) its diagonals must be perpendicular and must bisect each other. The point from the mathematician's perspective is that the properties follow from the definition, regardless of who does the proving. At a more elementary level, it doesn't matter who counts a finite set of objects or what culture that person belongs to. The answer will always be the same. (p. 6)

Alan H. Schoenfeld (1987) has explored themes related to mathematics' universality and cultural aspects. *If mathematics is free from cultural bias, why is there a discussion about teaching it to students from diverse cultural backgrounds? In other words, shouldn't the teaching methods also be culture-free if mathematics is indeed culture-free?*

You don't have to look very far to see how culture is interwoven in math materials, pedagogy, and assessment. My son was invited to take an IQ test in a public school in the ninth grade. In his book *IQ Testing 101*, Kaufman (2009) explains IQ tests are supposed to be designed so that studying for them has little effect on the actual score achieved. After taking the test, my son was frustrated that we did not prepare for the test. As a result, he was deeply concerned about his answer to one of the math problems because he did not know what a strawberry shortcake was. The word *short* impacted his perception of the problem. I could not have imagined the cultural expectations of the math question. The problem cited a culturally framed example that could not have been discernible by students who did not grow up encountering the multiple versions of strawberry shortcake. Math learning is not manipulating cold, sterile numbers on a page without cultural context. At its heart, it is a way of understanding the world. As such, it is natural for learners to use their cultural lenses to understand universal concepts such as a square. These lenses are mainly shaped by their backgrounds, including culture, language, and identities. As a discipline, mathematical ideas have been formed by cultural experiences and evolved through intercultural interactions (Joseph, 2000).

SHIFTING DEMOGRAPHICS

A report by Fabina et al. (2023) published by the U.S. Census Bureau examines changes in the racial/ethnic distribution of public school students in the demographic composition of U.S. public schools. In 2021, 49.4 million students were enrolled in public elementary and secondary schools. Following are the compositions according to race/ethnicity:

Race/Ethnicity	Population
White	22,400,000
Hispanic	14,100,000
Black	7,400,000
Asian	2,700,000
Two or more races	2,300,000
American Indian/Alaska Native	500,000
Pacific Islander	182,000

Source: NCES Racial/Ethnic Enrollment in Public Schools, 2023

From a pedagogical perspective, mathematics education has yet to reach its aim of personalizing learning experiences. The Eurocentric math education system struggles to create learning environments that expand to include multicultural lenses; it has historically relied on standardized testing and a linear teaching approach, implementing a one-size-fits-all method for teaching and assessing mathematical proficiency. This framework neglects cultural diversity and perpetuates racial disparities in educational outcomes (Yglesias, 2018).

The world is constantly culturally intersecting and even more so today. The Internet, travel, education, and connective social and commercial pathways inevitably lead to intercultural interactions and transformations: Gadgets and increasing Internet connectivity crisscross cultures in mega-highways of virtual social interaction. Intercultural dynamics form new versions of 21st-century cultural practices, objects, perspectives, and ideas. As a result, while cultures differ, similarities in how people live, learn, and work worldwide are increasingly ubiquitous.

Students' lunchboxes in U.S. schools contain a diverse array of international foods, such as dim sum, noodles, rice, burritos, barbecue, sandwiches, pasta, adobo, and more. Curiosity naturally entices children to explore and appreciate their peers' cuisines. This exemplifies how informal social peer interactions among children cultivate intercultural tapestries.

In response to the evolving socioeconomic landscape of the 21st century, the objectives of mathematics education must be redefined to ensure relevance. To address the significant implications of culture in mathematics, we must consider what and how we teach. Toward this end, the NCTM published *Professional Standards for Teaching Mathematics* (1991) and *Assessment Standards for School Mathematics* (1995), which reframed the teaching of mathematics and emphasized the importance of culture in math learning. The NCTM's position paper "The Intersection of Culture and Mathematics" (2024) underscores that

- Mathematics is not culturally neutral.
- Effective mathematics instruction leverages cultural knowledge and lived experiences as assets.
- Effective mathematics teachers are culturally aware.
- Effective schools develop systemic approaches that embrace culturally relevant mathematics instruction.

In our globalized world, diverse perspectives represent varied ways of seeing, understanding, and engaging. These intersections foster the creation of new ideas, strategies, and multidimensional viewpoints. The social dynamics presented in the math stories depict a world where mathematical learning is shaped by today's diverse classrooms representing multicultural children. Intercultural mathematical thinking arises when we recognize the development of a collective understanding of perceptions, ideas, methods, and questions that emerge from interconnected cultures. The universality of mathematical concepts and the multicultural pathways of math stories make dynamic and intercultural learning experiences possible.

EXPERIENCE

Making New Colors

Materials:

- Watercolors
- Paintbrushes
- Art paper

Steps:

1. Use any watercolor palette. Dip the brush into water and choose any color. Dab and brush onto the art paper.
2. Rinse the brush and choose another color. Dab and brush onto the art paper—partly color on top of the first color.
3. Mix and match colors.

> **Reflect:**
>
> - How does the experience reflect the transformative nature of intercultural learning?
>
> Blending colors produces new hues. Children's sociocultural backgrounds are like colors and lenses, shaping their self-perception and views of their surroundings.

INTERCULTURAL MATH STORIES

Our approach to developing math stories as an intercultural pedagogy is predicated on achieving the following objectives:

1. Building on children's innate mathematical abilities.
2. Cultivating curiosity, creativity, and community as intrinsic wellsprings and motivators for children's mathematical learning.
3. Addressing the diverse needs of multicultural children by emphasizing connection, engagement, and empowerment.
4. Shifting the focus of mathematics education from procedural algorithms to fostering mathematical sensemaking and reasoning.

If we want children to engage in mathematical sensemaking, learning mathematics must be meaningful. Empowering children is only possible in inclusive learning environments that embrace cultural diversity and promote genuine, collaborative efforts among students from varied backgrounds (Jones & Lee, 2018). Engaging children by building on their background knowledge and acknowledging their unique cultural perspectives also helps to prevent math anxiety. Children learn best when they feel safe and valued in an environment that acknowledges multiple viewpoints and explores diverse possibilities. A cooperative learning process with multiple access points nurtures a positive and engaged community of learners.

Observe how these students engage in the math activity. The math story shifted students' attitudes from *fear* of making mistakes to *excitement* and *confidence in their ability* to contribute knowledge, abilities, and insights to open-ended mathematical discovery and exploration.

MATHEMATICS IS AN ONGOING INTERCULTURAL HUMAN INVENTION

Interculturalism invites everybody to avoid all confinement phenomena by offering new opportunities for multiple interpretations and unexpected discoveries.

—UNESCO (2013)

Former UNESCO Director-General Irina Georgieva Bokova calls on everyone to promote a positive vision of cultural pluralism through learning, exchanges, and dialogue. Globalization shrinks the world and brings people of different cultural backgrounds closer together. Cultural diversity and intercultural connections are realities of modern life. The goal of intercultural learning is to bridge differences and promote intercultural dialogue. Interculturalism can be seen as part of a broad toolkit of worldviews, attitudes, and competencies that young people acquire for their lifelong journey.

Culture encompasses shared beliefs, customs, values, behaviors, traditions, and norms that characterize a particular group of people (Hofstede, 2001). It involves the way of life, including language, religion, cuisine, social interactions, art, music, and rituals, passed down from generation to generation

(Kroeber & Kluckhohn, 1952). Culture shapes individuals' identities and influences their perceptions, attitudes, and behaviors, guiding interactions within communities and the broader society (Schein, 2010). Cultural diversity arises from diverse cultures worldwide, contributing to the rich tapestry of human experience and heritage.

Math is not solely a European invention. Historically, universal mathematics is a bridge between cultures through the sharing of diverse ideas and processes. Social dynamics in historical contexts, scientific discoveries, human ingenuity, and the sheer necessity to survive against all odds influenced the advancement of mathematics. Using Darwin's (1859) simple definition of natural selection as an analogy, namely the process by which organisms best adapt to their surroundings, mathematics is a set of quantitative, spatial, and logical expressions, ideas, and processes that won historical practical and conceptual battles among mathematical practitioners, teachers, and theorists from all over the world.

MULTICULTURAL THREADS THAT WEAVE THE TAPESTRY OF MATHEMATICS: A BRIEF HISTORY

Understanding the historical development of mathematical ideas provides students, teachers, and parents with a deeper appreciation of the multiple influences that shaped the field vis-á-vis its relevance to the evolution of human civilization. Exploring the historical roots of mathematical concepts can help students develop a more robust understanding of the discipline and its real-world applications (Katz & Imhausen, 2007; Roth, 2003).

The Beginnings of Mathematical Practice

Evidence shows that humans have utilized mathematical concepts in various forms for thousands of years around the world. Early mathematical artifacts, such as tally marks on bones and artifacts related to measuring and surveying, have been found at archaeological sites. For example, the Ishango bone, discovered in the Democratic Republic of Congo and estimated to be over 20,000 years old, contains tally marks representing counting and numerical concepts (Schultz, 1981).

Mathematicians vary in their interpretations of ancient evidence of mathematical practice. Anthropologist Caleb Everett (2017) interprets the Ishango bone, suggesting that "the quantities evident in the groupings of marks are not random" and possibly indicate examples of prehistoric numerals. He proposes that the first column might exhibit a "doubling pattern," implying that the tool was used for counting and multiplication and possibly as a "numeric reference table." However, mathematician Olivier Keller cautions against imposing modern numerical concepts onto the Ishango bone. In contrast, Dirk Huylebrouck (2019), in his review of the research, supports the notion that the Ishango bone had an advanced mathematical function, asserting that "whatever the interpretation, the patterns surely show the bone was more than a simple tally stick" (1996, p. 58).

The discovery of the Ishango bone refutes a history of mathematics often presented through a Western-centric lens. Western bias has led to the underappreciation and marginalization of the contributions of non-Western mathematicians (Dixit & Ndlovu-Gatsheni, 2019).

While ancient Greek mathematicians made foundational contributions, the development of mathematics is a global story enriched by diverse influences and remarkable individuals (Smith, 2024). Historically, early contributions were generated by civilizations including Mesopotamia, India, China, and the Islamic world. These societies developed sophisticated mathematical systems, including algebra, geometry, and trigonometry, which profoundly influenced the evolution of basic and advanced mathematics.

A more inclusive understanding of mathematical history is essential (Katz & Imhausen, 2000). The intercultural evolution of modern mathematics refers to the intersections of mathematical ideas, concepts, and techniques across different cultures and civilizations throughout history. These interactions are dynamic, with mathematical knowledge flowing among multicultural societies, influencing and enriching each other's mathematical traditions.

Ancient Mathematics

Rhind Mathematical Papyrus, c. 2000 BCE.

Source: https://commons.wikimedia.org/wiki/File:Rhind_Mathematical_Papyrus.jpg

The foundations of modern mathematics trace their roots to ancient civilizations such as Mesopotamia, Egypt, Greece, India, China, and the Islamic world. Lumpkin (1987) underscores the significant mathematical contributions of Africa. Some mathematics historians assert that the discipline originated in Greece around 580 BCE, which is nearly 2,000 years after the advent of documented Egyptian mathematics. These historians often dismiss earlier mathematics as not being "true mathematics" due to the absence of formal, deductive proofs (Lumpkin, 1987, p. 4). However, the mathematics developed by the 13th century, upon which Western theories were later built, was more extensive than many scholars recognize. The rich mathematical heritage includes the Babylonian right triangle theorem, Chinese contributions such as the triangle and negative numbers, the Indo-Arabic numeral system including the concept of zero as a placeholder, Al-Khwarizmi's algebra, the Mayan use of zero as a placeholder and base 20 numerals, the navigational geometry developed by Pacific Islanders, and the mathematical principles embedded in people's art.

For instance, around 5,000 years ago, the geometry of ancient Egypt was mainly developed to survey and measure land along the Nile River for agricultural purposes. The Egyptians applied basic geometric principles to divide land plots, establish boundaries, and calculate areas. The Rhind papyrus, also referred to as the Ahmose or British papyrus (Calinger, 1995), is a mathematics textbook written approximately in 1650 BCE by the Egyptian scribe Ahmes. As a mathematical guide book with tables and problems, scribes utilized it to learn how to solve mathematical challenges (Millmore, 2016).

Mathematical Innovation of the Eastern Zhou Dynasty

1	2	3	4	5	6	7	8	9
I	II	III	IIII	IIIII	T	TT	TTT	TTTT

Source: Seijutsu Sangaku Zue, 1795. A Japanese counting board. An illustration of Chinese counting rods. Digits in counting rods and counting board are equivalent to distinct place values.

In *A History of Chinese Mathematics*, Jean-Claude Martzloff provides an in-depth exploration of the history of mathematics in China. During the ancient Chinese dynasties, such as the Zhou, Qin, and Han dynasties, from 1046 BCE to 220 CE, Chinese mathematicians invented the decimal system and the concept of zero and developed algorithms for arithmetic operations. They also made advancements in geometry, particularly in measuring angles, areas, and volumes.

Intersecting cultures in the Silk Roads made significant contributions to mathematics in East–West and North–South societies. This includes elaborations and applications of arithmetic, geometry, algebra, and trigonometry. Trade routes are pivotal in exchanging goods and sharing ideas across cultures. The vast and historic network of both land and sea routes connected China with the Mediterranean, bridging diverse civilizations with various cultures, religions, and languages. This extensive intercultural interaction facilitated the exchange of knowledge, technical expertise, and friendships, creating a lasting legacy of connectivity and cultural appreciation.

Transmission of Mathematical Knowledge

In his book *The Silk Roads: A New History of the World*, Frankopan (2015) explains how numerous cities along the Silk Road, spanning China, Central Asia, Arabia, India, Persia, and Turkey, led to significant economic growth and cultural exchange across various regions. The wealth generated from trade spurred advancements in industrial processes such as printing, glassmaking, and papermaking, as well as in fields like medicine, philosophy, astronomy, and agriculture. These cities became dynamic hubs that attracted intellectual polymaths, leaving a profound and enduring impact on the historical record.

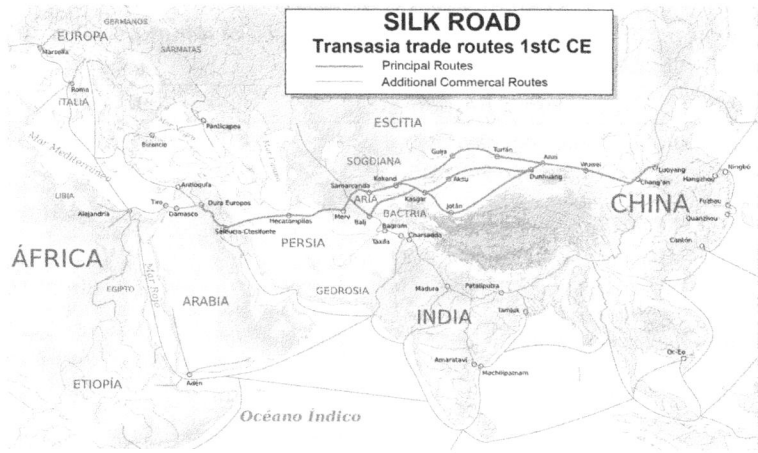

Source: https://commons.wikimedia.org/wiki/File:Silk_Road_in_the_I_century_AD_-_ru.svg# /media/File:Silk_Road_in_the_I_century_AD_-_es.svg

Silk Roads, the Indian Ocean trade routes, and other networks facilitated the transmission of mathematical knowledge between civilizations. Scholars, traders, and travelers exchanged mathematical ideas, texts, and techniques, leading to the intercultural fertilization of mathematical concepts. The spread of mathematical knowledge along trade routes and through cultural exchanges facilitated the exchange of ideas between civilizations (Katz & Imhausen, 2007).

Islamic Mathematics

During the Islamic Golden Age (8th to 14th centuries), scholars in the Islamic world made remarkable advances in mathematics, preserving and expanding upon Greek, Indian, and Persian mathematical knowledge.

Mathematical virtuosos such as Al-Khwarizmi, Al-Kindi, and Ibn al-Haytham considerably contributed to algebra, trigonometry, and geometry. Islamic mathematicians made groundbreaking advancements in algebra, trigonometry, and geometry, preserving and expanding upon mathematical knowledge from diverse sources (O'Connor & Robertson, 2000). The Latin translation of Muhammad ibn Musa al-Khwarizmi's works reveals how much of Europe's mathematics was based on his writings and those of other Islamic mathematicians. The words *algorithm* and *algebra* are derived from his writings.

To illustrate Al-Khwarizmi's methods, consider the following math problem, which requires completing the square. Compare Al-Khwarizmi's solution (quoted in Corry, 2025) with the modern algebra equivalent.

Question: What is the value of *X* if the square of a number plus 10 times the number equals 39?

Al-Khwarizmi's Response	Modern Algebra
You halve the number of roots, which in the present instance yields 5.	Rewrite the equation:
	$x^2 + 10x = 39$
This you multiply by itself; the product is 25. Add this to 39; the sum is 64.	Complete the square:
	$x^2 + 10x + 25 = 39 + 25$
Now take the root of this, which is 8, and subtract from it half the number of the roots, which is 5; the remainder is 3.	Simplify:
	$(x + 5)^2 = 64$
This is the root of the square which you sought.	Solve for x:
	Take the square root of both sides:
	$x + 5 = \pm 8$
	Subtract 5 from both sides:
	$x = 3$ or $x = -13$

Medieval Europe

A page from the *Liber Abaci* (Latin meaning Book of Calculation) containing the first 13 numbers of the Fibonacci sequence.

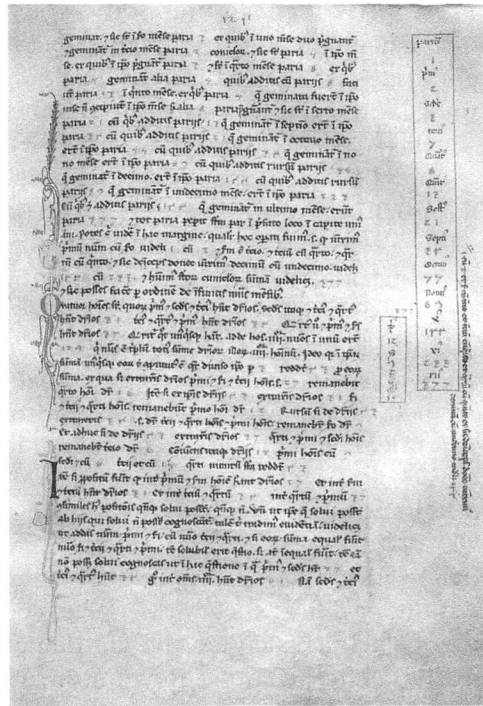

Source: https://commons.wikimedia.org/wiki/File:Liber_abbaci_magliab_f124r.jpg

Islamic mathematics profoundly influenced medieval Europe, with translations of Arabic mathematical texts sparking a revival of mathematical learning in Europe. In his book *The Man of Numbers: Fibonacci's Arithmetic Revolution*, Devlin (2011) elucidates how Leonardo da Pisa's *Liber Abaci* acted as a catalyst for the transmission of Islamic mathematical knowledge to Europe, primarily through the introduction and popularization of the Hindu–Arabic numeral system and algebraic techniques, which he learned from Arabic sources during his travels in North Africa and the Mediterranean region.

The contributions of Greek mathematicians played a pivotal role in shaping the development of mathematics as a discipline. They formulated and wrote theoretical concepts and emphasized the importance of rigorous deductive reasoning and proof in mathematics. These historical documents laid the groundwork for today's mathematical principles and techniques (Merzbach & Boyer, 2011).

Pythagoras and his followers explored the properties of numbers and geometric figures, leading to the Pythagorean theorem. Archimedes contributed significantly to calculus, integral calculus, and calculating geometric shapes' areas and volumes. Euclid laid the foundations of geometry in his seminal work, *Elements*. Euclid's systematic approach to geometry included developing axioms and proofs.

Euclid's *Elements*, written around 300 BCE, is a seminal work that laid the foundations of geometry and systematically presents a series of geometric principles, definitions, postulates, and propositions. Covering various topics, including plane geometry, solid geometry, number theory, and the theory of proportions, Euclid's work provided a comprehensive treatise on geometry. It served as a model for mathematical reasoning and proof that influenced mathematical thought for centuries.

The concept of zero and its incorporation into the numeral system was developed over time and through the contributions of various cultures. In ancient Indian mathematics, particularly in texts dating back to around the 5th century CE and later, such as the *Brahmasphutasiddhanta* by the Indian mathematician and astronomer Brahmagupta, we see the explicit use of zero as a numerical digit. Brahmagupta describes arithmetic operations involving zero and rules for dealing with zero in mathematical calculations.

Renaissance and Beyond

During the Renaissance, Europe experienced a vibrant surge in mathematical exploration. Visionary minds such as Descartes, Fermat, and Newton pushed the boundaries of algebra, calculus, and mathematical physics with their pioneering discoveries. The Scientific Revolution then spurred an even faster evolution of modern mathematics, introducing novel methods and fields of study that continue to shape our understanding of today's world.

The Mathematics of Hardware and Software

Modern mathematics has seen significant growth, with a strong emphasis on abstract and theoretical advancements. Fields such as set theory, abstract algebra, topology, and mathematical logic have made remarkable progress as mathematicians explore increasingly complex structures and ideas.

Mathematical physics underwent a significant transformation with the advent of theories like relativity and quantum mechanics. Albert Einstein's theory of relativity introduced new mathematical concepts such as non-Euclidean geometry and tensor calculus. Simultaneously, quantum mechanics required sophisticated mathematical tools to describe the probabilistic events occurring at the atomic and subatomic levels.

The mid-20th century spawned digital machines with powerful software, driving the development of computational mathematics and computer science. Mathematicians began to explore algorithms, numerical methods, and computational techniques to simulate intricate systems and solve complex mathematical problems. They laid the foundation for modern computer-based mathematical analysis and modeling during this period.

Today, modern mathematics thrives on interdisciplinary partnerships, with mathematicians working closely with scientists, engineers, and researchers across various fields. These collaborations have led to groundbreaking discoveries and innovations, advancing cryptography, data science, and mathematical physics.

Globalization has further facilitated the exchange of mathematical knowledge worldwide. International collaborations, conferences, and publications allow mathematicians from diverse cultures to share ideas and advance the field.

Connecting math learning to contexts will help children understand how these theorems were developed. For most of what is taught at elementary grade levels, the math ideas and procedures emanated from creating ways to calculate for socioeconomic and political purposes. Hartnett and Koepfle (2011) recommend engaging middle-school students in understanding the mathematics of the Rhind papyrus. While modern-day mathematicians may question the accuracy of this approach, ancient Egyptians used visual tools and estimation, providing another lens through which to learn how to calculate the area of a circle.

When students are invited to develop mathematical ideas, they gain a deeper appreciation for the subject. Rather than learning through memorizing facts and formulas, mathematical thinking involves understanding the context and reasoning behind mathematical concepts (Smith, 2019). This approach invites critical thinking and deeper engagement with mathematics. We are human, after all. Moreover, contextual applications prepare students for transfer. They learn by generalizing from a context and recognizing how math ideas and processes work in various historical contexts.

EXPERIENCE

Grandparents' Different Ways of Cooking Rice

Materials:

- Uncooked rice grains
- Water
- Rice cooking tools

> **Steps:**
>
> 1. For teachers: Ask your students to ask their grandparents how they measure when cooking rice.
>   For parents: Ask any older relative or neighbor how they measure when cooking rice.
> 2. How does their method of measuring quantity, heat levels, and cooking time affect the quality of cooked rice?
>
> **Reflect:**
>
> - What do the responses say about one's culture, math, and its application to cooking rice?

Every culture has its way of measuring and applying quantifiable variables when cooking rice. How have the varied approaches come about? How can we tell if one is better than the other?

Exposing children to these differences will open their minds to how our backgrounds shape our thinking. You may even want to do a rice-cooking activity in class!

CLASSROOM RICE-MAKING ACTIVITY

1. Group students from similar cultural backgrounds and invite grandparents who can guide them in their rice-cooking adventures.
2. Focus on the mathematics of the rice-cooking recipe or methods for measuring.
3. Have the children taste cooked rice from each of the groups.
4. Guide them in determining their criteria for what well-cooked rice is.
5. Discuss the variety of approaches and what this means for math learning.

METACOGNITION AND THE CULTURAL LENS

Increasing children's awareness of how their backgrounds and cultural lenses influence their thoughts and feelings about mathematical ideas and activities develops metacognitive skills in math learning. In the big picture, knowing how culture affects their thinking makes them aware of the invisible lenses that impact how they see, participate in, and feel about the world. When children are encouraged to value their unique backgrounds and learn from one another's differing views and methods, they gain intercultural learning and understanding competencies.

MULTICULTURAL INTERSECTIONS IN MATH EDUCATION

> According to UNESCO (2020), schools are central to nurturing intercultural competencies that involve navigating complex environments marked by diverse peoples, cultures, and lifestyles. In other words, the ability to perform "effectively and appropriately when interacting with others linguistically and culturally different from oneself." (Fantini, 2006)

Shifting the narrative and acknowledging contributions beyond Western perspectives acknowledges the breadth and depth of mathematical achievements across cultures. The intercultural evolution of modern mathematics highlights the universal fabric of mathematical traditions and the enriching exchange of ideas across cultures (Joseph, 1991). This accentuates how diversity and intercultural collaboration shape mathematics as a global discipline.

The universal nature of mathematics, which involves concepts and methods of thinking quantitatively, made it possible to achieve an East–West and North–South integration. Intercultural learning is an element of empathy. Intercultural competencies free people from their logic and cultural idioms to engage with others and listen to their ideas.

Embracing cultural diversity in mathematics education enriches students' learning experiences. Recognizing and appreciating multicultural lenses reflected in the pedagogy and problem-solving activities that build upon students' varied perspectives and abilities makes mathematics more inclusive and accessible for all learners. This is what the rice activity represents. It makes math learning meaningful in the classroom and alive at home with the family.

CREATIVE INTEGRATION OF RESEARCH INTO MATH STORIES

To begin our research, we interviewed primary school teachers about math learning in Guatemala and the United States. Guatemala's low mathematics performance, as reflected in its Programme for International Student Assessment (PISA) scores, led directors from three schools to seek help in creating effective math learning solutions for their students. From interviews, we learned that many primary school teachers were traumatized by their math educational experiences. As a result, many subject teachers avoided discussing anything related to math. The fear of math among both teachers and parents was palpable in the conversations. Very few claimed they were good at math, emphasizing that their ability to memorize math facts and algorithms was crucial for passing the subject tests.

MATH STORIES CAN CATALYZE INTERCULTURAL MATH LEARNING

The findings of the study's first phase fueled the creation of intercultural math stories. The intercultural framework evolved from the cultural imitations posed by mainstream math education. To improve math proficiency across varied student populations with multicultural backgrounds, an alternative necessitated addressing elements that alienate students from connecting with mathematics. The pedagogy has to reframe from the Eurocentric framework, insufficient contextualization, and a one-size-fits-all approach.

The challenge we faced was how intercultural elements could weave mathematical concepts with what we've called hybrid cultural themes reflective of the 21st century or mixed cultures in simulations of real-world applications. The narratives must be designed to make math both accessible and relevant, showcasing how math can be accessible in a classroom of multicultural students of diverse abilities learning through an intercultural process.

THE IMPERFECT TOWN OF WHATEVER

> Architectural differences in buildings around the globe both tell and preserve the story of humanity.
>
> —Avanti Systems (n.d.)

During our interviews, we noticed discussions about math frequently concluded with the dismissive term *Whatever!* When asked what they meant, the teachers shrugged their shoulders or remarked, *It's just that, whatever!*

Taking off from the interviews, the fictional *Town of Whatever* evolved. The *Dictionary Britannica* defines the word *whatever* as (1) anything or everything; (2) no matter what, regardless of what; (3) used in questions that express surprise or confusion; and (4) informal definition is what not or anything. To us, the word expresses how learning happens in the stories—where children explore possibilities through mathematical interactions in a fictional world they can call their own.

EXPERIENCE

An Intercultural Town

Materials:

- Computer/tablet
- Web access

Steps:

1. Observe the elements of the Town of Whatever. What are the cultural influences?
2. Download a world map from the Internet and copy/paste this on a slide presentation.
3. Mark the countries you believe are the sources of the design elements.

Reflect:

- How does the architectural design reflect children's everyday interactions and environments?
- How can you use the world map and the Town of Whatever picture to discuss children's multicultural and intercultural characteristics?

Pictures and colors convey multitudes, especially in children's books. The text–picture relationship is how the text and pictures interact and build upon each other. It is the synergy of words and images (Sipe, 1998). Synergy is the production by two or more agents, substances, or other factors of a combined effect more significant than the sum of their separate effects. Using math stories, students can engage in math concepts through the language, the story, but importantly also the images.

INTERCULTURAL SCENE DESIGNS

The architectural design of the *Town of Whatever* simulates today's evolving visual multicultural world of young learners, enriched by intercultural connections. The intentional aesthetics in these illustrations aim to inspire children to see their environments with an intercultural aesthetic sensibility. We envision a modern, culturally intersectional, transforming world by integrating cultures through design. In the stories you choose for your students, or the ones you and your students create together, think about how the images convey the cultural diversity of your students and the world they inhabit.

INSIGHTS FROM THE FIELD

How children learn significantly impacts their feelings and perceptions of mathematics. Our studies with children in grades K–1 demonstrate that math stories can transform fear of mathematics into positive engagement and curiosity. These stories are crafted with creative narratives, characters, and culturally inclusive situations, providing personalized invitations to children from diverse backgrounds. This approach acknowledges that each child's unique cultural lens plays a crucial role in their learning process.

As a result of this story-driven learning environment, children shifted from apprehension to forming positive associations with mathematics, engaging authentically with the content. The intercultural interactions encouraged by the stories enhanced the learning atmosphere and excited the children when asked to produce mathematical solutions. They were enthusiastic and eager to contribute their ideas, taking pride in their newfound ability to reason mathematically. One student wanted the math stories to continue indefinitely, saying, "I wish this math story would last forever."

Children's cultural backgrounds act like lenses, shaping their self-perceptions and interpretations of the world around them. In our increasingly globalized society, these diverse lenses represent different ways of seeing, understanding, and engaging with content. The interactions among multicultural children and their families lead to rich intercultural exchanges and open up creative possibilities for learning. These multidimensional intersections foster innovative problem-solving methods and deepen the children's understanding of mathematical concepts. This holistic approach enriches children's mathematical knowledge and prepares them to thrive in a diverse world.

CHAPTER 4

Relatable Characters Bring Math to Life

If a story is not about the hearer, he will not listen. And here I make a rule—a great and interesting story is about everyone or it will not last.

—John Steinbeck, *East of Eden*

EXPERIENCE

Your Favorite Character (Part 1)

What better way is there to explore the importance of characters than by reflecting on your own favorite fictional character from your childhood?

Activity:

On a sheet, write a couple of points on the following:

- Their physical appearance
- Their personality
- Their family and friends
- Their hobbies and interests
- Any other notable features

If you're feeling artsy, draw the character next to the descriptors!
Finally, write a few points on why they were your favorite character.

Reflect:

- What was your character's story about?
- What did you learn from that story and from that character?
- What made the character relatable to you?
- How do your favorite character's traits relate to what makes a character effective in learning math?
- What do you think children can learn from characters like this?

HUMANIZING MATH THROUGH CHARACTERS

From ancient oral traditions like *Anansi the Spider* to the ancient literary work, *The Epic of Gilgamesh*, to Western classics such as Shakespeare's *Hamlet*, characters lie at the heart of stories across all cultures, reflecting what Steven Pinker (1997) describes as a feature of our "universal psychology." As Kendall Haven (2007) emphasizes in *Story Proof: The Science Behind the Startling Power of Story*, characters are essential to narratives because they provide context and relevance to the information being conveyed. Every piece of a story, from plot to setting, is anchored to a character. To illustrate this point as Haven does, try describing the story from the preceding Experience without mentioning any characters. How much meaning and information from the original is preserved?

In the context of learning, characters, of course, do more than drive the plot—they shape how children engage with and understand the world. They embody diverse experiences and perspectives and serve as emotional and cognitive bridges, transforming abstract ideas into more accessible narratives that resonate with young learners, making them easier to grasp.

In literature, according to Roser et al. (2007), characters can help guide readers through challenging thematic concepts and provide a relatable medium for learning valuable life lessons. By stepping into a character's shoes, readers process complex ideas in a more tangible way. Similarly, when mathematical concepts are framed through story characters, math comes alive. Children can project themselves into the struggles and triumphs of these characters as they face challenges that require applying math knowledge. Characters become models for navigating problems, which helps children see math as approachable and applicable to real-world scenarios (Keat & Wilburne, 2009; Trakulphadetkrai et al., 2019). By situating math within a narrative, characters offer a transformative personal connection that helps children see math not as a distant or rigid discipline but as an integral part of their everyday experiences.

This chapter will explore how characters facilitate math learning and comprehension, beginning with an in-depth examination of the mechanisms behind character-driven engagement. It will then address the crucial role of intercultural diversity and representation in fostering this engagement, creating inclusive learning environments that make math accessible and meaningful to all students.

HOW CHARACTERS ACTIVATE INTERNAL DRIVERS OF LEARNING

John Gardner aptly states in his timeless guide for young writers, *The Art of Fiction*, "The first thing that makes a reader read a story is that he cares about the characters." This emotional connection is the foundation of engagement, drawing readers—in this case, young learners—into the story by giving students a stake in the character's journey. Without this attachment, the math becomes another classroom concept to master, devoid of personal significance. But when students bond with a character, the problems that character faces become intertwined with their own emotional experience, encouraging a deeper involvement with math concepts in order to address the now meaningful challenges that serve the character's journey.

EMPATHY-DRIVEN ENGAGEMENT

Emotional connection's most profound impact lies in its ability to generate empathy. More than just an emotional resonance, empathy becomes a powerful tool for learning by transforming a character's challenges into something the student feels personally responsible for solving. This sense of companionship and solidarity places math within a broader narrative, where students become invested in the character's success. No longer solving abstract problems in isolation, they are helping a "friend" overcome real obstacles, making the learning process more purposeful.

*Maya writes an **equation** to explain the problem.*

Total buttons = Total buttonholes

She figures out how to use math to solve the problem!

Once empathy has taken root, a critical shift occurs—students begin to perceive math problem-solving not as a senseless exercise but as a necessity. In Casey's (2004) study, characters, represented by puppets in the classroom, became cherished by the children. Teachers reported that these puppets were treated as if they were part of the class, with students spontaneously incorporating them into other learning activities on their own. These characters became significant motivators for children to engage with the math material to help solve their problems because the characters relied on the children's help. This sense of responsibility, derived from empathy, makes the learning process emotionally and personally compelling.

From there, the empathy-driven sense of responsibility sparks curiosity and creativity, prompting an active search for solutions. Keat and Wilburne's (2009) study similarly found that children became deeply involved with the characters, integrating them in dramatic play, drawing, and writing. The characters foster imaginative thinking in mathematics. Initially, children approached the characters' problems as if they were real, leading them to experiment through guessing, estimation, and creative strategies. As they continued, they transitioned from imaginative problem-solving to more concrete mathematical approaches yet continued to engage through the lens of the storybook characters.

IT ALL STARTS WITH RELATABILITY

Creating emotional connections with characters is not merely about making the story interesting or creating a likable character, however; a truly strong connection requires relatability—the capacity to see oneself in the character. If emotional connection is the anchor that holds the reader's interest and empathy is the engine that drives genuine engagement, then relatability is the hook that draws them in in the first place.

Ruby is an ice cream maker. Her profession aligns with a popular dessert among children, making the profession relatable. A black lady with pink hair and clogs inspires children to express their unique selves.

When children identify with characters with characteristics or experiences similar to their own, they are drawn into the narrative on a deeper emotional level. Bal and Veltkamp's study (2013) reinforces this idea, finding that when readers identify with characters, their capacity for empathy heightens, as the identification enables them to experience the thoughts, emotions, and struggles of the characters as if they were their own. Conversely, if readers fail to connect or sympathize with characters, they may disengage, diminishing their empathic responses.

THE RELATABILITY RECIPE

Relatability can be built through a thoughtful blend of *personality, individual experiences, cultural background, socioeconomic context*, and *problem-solving approaches*. Acknowledging these diverse factors is vital to understanding how students perceive and interact with both math and the broader world around them. The more dimensions we consider, the more inclusive the learning process becomes, providing multiple entry points for a greater variety of learners. Additionally, the visual design of characters in picture books plays a pivotal role in fostering relatability. The way characters are drawn—their facial expressions, body language, and interactions with their environment—significantly influences how children perceive and connect with them.

In our *MathXplorers* book series, characters are deliberately crafted to align their unique personalities, interests, and talents with specific approaches to math problem-solving, with their visual design further enhancing these traits. Like other educational series—such as *Little Einsteins*, *The Magic School Bus*, or even *Dora the Explorer*, with her pan-Latina identity—*MathXplorers* offers racial diversity in skin tone without explicitly assigning ethnicity or culture. This allows a broader range of students to project themselves onto the characters, creating a sense of inclusivity without limiting relatability to specific cultural experiences. For each character, the combination of attributes aims to break away from or subvert common stereotypes and tropes, while modeling and affirming students' varied intellectual and personal backgrounds.

To illustrate the various factors that contribute to a character's relatability, here's a breakdown of the attributes of the main characters of our *MathXplorers* book series:

- *Bikoy* approaches math through patterns and equations, favoring algorithmic or algebraic methods. Bikoy's appearance—a collared polo, a messenger bag, and shorts, combined with his neatly buzzed hair—reflects his mature, collected demeanor, while his practical and patient nature reflects the supportive, understanding peer-tutor, countering stereotypes of the arrogant math whiz.
- *Amyel* connects math to the world around him through a visual and graphic approach, often incorporating shapes and drawings into his problem-solving. His imaginative and whimsical personality brings a sense of creativity and fun to the learning process, with illustrations often showing him floating among geometric shapes. Amyel's wild, curly hair contrasts with his more formal attire, imbuing authenticity into his character.
- *Iliana* embodies a kinetic approach to math, where movement and physical activity are integral to her problem-solving. Her spirited, enthusiastic nature is complemented by an outfit fitting her active lifestyle: a tank top and shorts that allow her freedom to move and dance. Typically depicted with limbs akimbo, Iliana offers a relatable role model for students who may not fit into the traditional, sedentary mold of math learning.
- *Misha* takes an eclectic approach to math, blending finger-counting, tallying, and a curious "what if?" mindset. This mixed style makes Misha the most empathetic of the group, meeting others where they are in their mathematical journey. His casual yet motley appearance, with mixed patterns and colors, reflects his multifaceted approach to problem-solving, resonating with students who feel they don't fit neatly into conventional categories.

By offering distinct appearances, personalities, and problem-solving styles, *MathXplorers* creates multiple pathways into math. This ensures that students of various interests and backgrounds can find characters they can meaningfully connect with, allowing them to access both the narrative and the math concepts. This representation empowers students to explore math in ways that reflect their own experiences, making the learning process more enriching for everyone.

EXPERIENCE

Your Favorite Character (Part 2)

Now, let's combine your favorite character with mathematical thinking and problem-solving.

Steps:

1. Come up with a math problem within a real-world context.
2. Think about how each of the four MathXplorers would approach the problem. What ideas, methods, or tools would they use?
3. Illustrate their approach. Stick figures are ok!
4. Next, refer back to the characteristics from Part 1 and think about how your favorite character would approach the problem.
5. Illustrate their approach.

Reflect:

- What characteristics of your favorite character made you feel that they would take such a problem-solving approach?
- Which approach did you personally connect with the most and why?
- How might the five characters work together to come up with a solution? How might their ideas build off of one another?

MIRRORS AND WINDOWS: THE IMPORTANCE OF DIVERSE CHARACTERS

While cultural diversity in children's books has improved in recent years, there is still considerable progress to be made. According to the Cooperative Children's Book Center annual diversity statistics, 40% of books published in 2023 featured at least one Black, Indigenous, or person of color (BIPOC) primary character or human subject, based on a sample of 3,491 books. This represents a notable increase from 2018, the inaugural year of data collection, when only 27% of books included BIPOC representation in a main figure; however, it is only a 1% increase from 2022, indicating a plateau in growth (SLJ Staff, 2024). This trend underscores the need for continued efforts to prioritize diverse representation in children's literature.

Moreover, many of the books surveyed focus on specific racial or cultural themes, while stories portraying children of color engaging in everyday activities—especially those involving mathematical thinking—are still rare (Kliman, 2019). For example, most math books on the market feature animals, objects, or white children as the primary subjects, further highlighting the gap in culturally diverse representations in mathematics literature.

For books to truly humanize and properly contextualize math, the characters must reflect the diversity of experiences and backgrounds present in our increasingly globalized world. Drawing on Rudine Sims Bishop's (1990) metaphor, children's books offer both "mirrors" that reflect the reader's own identity and experiences and "windows" that provide a view into the lives of others. This dual function is pivotal in shaping students' understanding of themselves and the world around them (Crawford et al., 2024).

Diverse Characters Affirm, Inspire, and Empower Young Mathematicians

Diversity makes math more accessible, inclusive, and relevant. By presenting a variety of perspectives, these stories help students recognize the richness and variety of mathematical thinking (Livers & Karp, 2018). For students from underrepresented communities, representation in math stories is essential for affirming their identities and experiences, fostering a sense of belonging in the mathematical process. By connecting math to familiar contexts, diverse characters provide a bridge for students to explore concepts in ways that feel more intuitive, as students are more likely to build relationships with math when they are reflected in the stories they read (Robinson, 2023).

Jessica notices, "When 2 lines meet at a point, they also create a corner!"

"Yes!" answers Amyel. "**Triangles have 3 sides and 3 corners**."

Jessica connects abstract ideas, like a *point* in a triangle, to a *corner* in building structures. Her character is a natural cognitive bridge to making everyday objects and structures mathematically meaningful. Amyel exemplifies how one can build on children's background knowledge and ideas and elevate these to mathematical ideas.

Trakulphadetkrai et al. (2019) emphasize that children's literature read during formative years significantly influences how they form their self-concept and future potential. Without diverse characters in these stories, many students—especially girls and students of color—may feel excluded from the world of mathematics, reinforcing stereotypes about who can succeed in math. By presenting a more balanced and inclusive array of characters, math stories allow all students to see themselves as capable mathematicians (Livers & Karp, 2018).

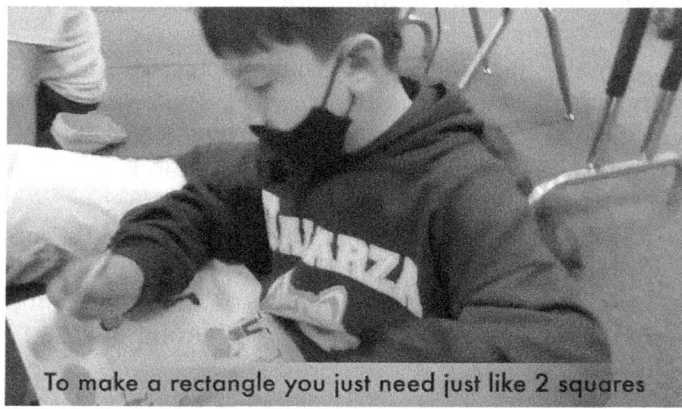

To make a rectangle you just need just like 2 squares

These character role models empower students to take ownership of their learning and become active participants in the mathematical meaning-making process. As Gutierrez (2018) asserts, this affirmation encourages students to draw from their own cultural and linguistic resources, enabling them to engage with math in ways that are authentic to their lived experiences.

In the above illustration, Teacher Rebecca used the poster to allow children to express their ideas and make visible individual contributions in many ways to make the number ten.

When students feel their identities are validated, they are more willing to explore math creatively rather than simply reproducing traditional algorithms or concepts. Math becomes a "living practice," full of debates, culture, and power, where students can safely and confidently innovate new mathematical approaches and think of math as a tool for solving real-world problems that matter to them.

Inclusive representation not only cultivates the critical, empathetic connections that power the internal drivers of learning but also builds students' confidence to engage with math on their own terms. By seeing characters who reflect their unique perspectives, students gain the confidence and agency to explore math as a tool for expressing their understanding of the world.

Diversity + Empathy = Community

For underrepresented students, seeing characters that mirror their own lives provides a sense of belonging in the math classroom, transforming a personal connection into a collective one. These students, who may often feel excluded in traditional school settings, come to view themselves as part of a diverse mathematical community where their unique perspectives and contributions matter, allowing them to engage more confidently in mathematical discussions (Robinson, 2023).

Diversity in math stories also helps build a stronger sense of community by eliciting empathy and prosocial behavior. When applied to a broader group or social context, identifying with characters in stories encourages students to extend empathy toward their peers. Research by Bal and Veltkamp (2013) suggests that when students identify with characters in stories and emotionally engage with them, they practice being empathic, which enhances their social-emotional growth, interpersonal skills, and prosocial behavior in real life.

Furthermore, Larsen et al. (2018) found that stories featuring human characters rather than animals improved children's comprehension of moral lessons and increased prosocial behavior, such as sharing. The researchers found this because children perceived human characters as more similar to themselves, allowing them to transfer the lessons from the story into their real lives. This demonstrates the potential for diverse characters to serve as models of behavior.

For white students, diverse representation in stories offers the opportunity to see their underrepresented peers as fully realized individuals, challenging stereotypes and promoting intercultural understanding. Robinson (2023) highlights how stories featuring diverse characters allow students to see beyond superficial labels and appreciate the complexity and individuality of others. These stories serve as models for intercultural interactions, showing students how to navigate diverse environments with respect and understanding.

By engaging empathy through diverse representation, these stories create a dynamic and inclusive classroom environment where students can learn to weave together and collectively build on their differences, participate in intercultural mathematical thinking, and pave the way for true collective meaning-making.

Intercultural Dynamics of Collective Meaning-Making

The ability to empathize with and understand others from different cultural backgrounds is critical for both personal and academic growth. The dynamics in math stories reflect the diversity of today's classrooms, where students bring varied perspectives, ideas, and methods to the table. Intercultural mathematical thinking emerges when students recognize that math is not a solitary endeavor but a collaborative process shaped by their diverse experiences, and by drawing on each other's perceptions and approaches, students can develop new strategies and solutions.

This intercultural interaction enriches mathematical learning by showing students that there is a multiplicity of problem-solving approaches. Diverse characters in math stories help bridge cultural and intellectual divides, offering insights into how different communities think about and engage with mathematical concepts. By recognizing the power of these varied perspectives, students can approach math with greater creativity and collaboration, understanding that the diversity within their classroom strengthens their collective problem-solving abilities.

Intercultural conversations sparked by these diverse narratives become rich intersections of languages, cultural references, and ideas, allowing students to see that there is no single path to solving a problem. Through the lens of intercultural math stories, students come to understand that the diversity of their classroom community is not just a reflection of the world outside—it is a powerful tool for learning and innovating within mathematics.

Here is a framework for analyzing the role of characters in math learning.

Table 4.1. Framework for Engaging Story Characters in Math Learning

Characters Inspire Agency in Math Learning	Students' Background Knowledge Are Wellsprings of Mathematical Understanding	Accessible and Challenging Sensemaking and Problem-Solving to Achieve Flow	Context-Driven Conceptual Understanding with Procedural Practice Leads to Transfer
Necessity			
Personal and Real-World Relevance	How do the characters make math learning relevant and compelling to children?	Are the characters placed in situations where they must use math to solve critical problems or overcome obstacles?	How do the characters inspire children to feel empowered by their mathematical abilities and see them as necessary tools for independence and success?
Curiosity			
Capturing and Sustaining Children's Interest	What intuitive approaches do the story's characters use to capture and sustain children's interest in learning math?	How do the characters model mathematical thinking and persistence and guide children in making sense of math concepts and problem-solving?	Do the characters ask intriguing, open-ended questions or present unstructured problems to encourage exploration of math ideas and procedures?

(continued)

Table 4.1. (continued)

Characters Inspire Agency in Math Learning	Students' Background Knowledge Are Wellsprings of Mathematical Understanding	Accessible and Challenging Sensemaking and Problem-Solving to Achieve Flow	Context-Driven Conceptual Understanding with Procedural Practice Leads to Transfer
Creativity			
Explore Multiple Pathways to Arrive at a Solution	Do the story characters inspire children to use their background knowledge to make sense of problems and figure out solutions?	How do the characters inspire inventive thinking and encourage children to see math as a flexible tool with hints or clues that connect with children's emotions or personal experiences?	How do the characters create opportunities for children to approach math learning through multiple perspectives—cultural, imaginative, or knowledge-based?
Community			
Valuing Cultural Lenses and Cooperative Learning	How do the characters in the story inspire children to value their cultural lenses in the context of intercultural learning?	How does the story promote cooperative thinking? Does the story reflect how math helps make sense of and create a better world?	How do the interactions among the characters showcase the dynamics of a positive and respectful community that values children as participants IN making a better world?

CHAPTER 5

Get Ready to Teach With Math Stories

EXPERIENCE

Algebraic Thinking: Find X

Steps:

This is an adaptation of the game called *Hot and Cold*.

1. An object will be hidden. When the object is unknown, it is called *X*. When it is found and known, it has a name. It can be any object, such as a pencil or a book.
2. Explain that an object, *X*, is hidden in the room. The children must find it, and whoever does, states its real name.
3. How will the children know where to find the object X? Ask them if they know the *Hot and Cold* game. Explain that when the teacher says *hot*, the children are moving close to the object. When the children are veering away from the object, s/he says, *cold*. The children look for the object. The teacher guides the search with the clues, *hot* and *cold*.
4. What happens when a child finds the object *X*? The child says *X is* and then states the object's name. Then, this child gets to hide the following object as the other children close their eyes. The cycle continues with hiding, searching for *X*, and identifying *X* = the object.
5. Children reflect on the activity. After finding five objects, the teacher instructs the class to form a circle and reflect on the activity. *How did it feel to hide and look for the objects? What did X signify? What happens to X when we find the object?*

Reflect:

- How does the game introduce *algebraic thinking*?

The game introduces algebraic thinking in a fun simulation of *X = unknown*. The dynamics of play set the tone for an equal playing field among children. The game requires participation from all students. They engage in social interactions

---

following game rules. Students are physically, socially, and cognitively energized. Physical and social activities are wellsprings for conceptual understanding. Moreover, play is fun and can trigger the release of endorphins, the body's natural feel-good chemicals.

MATH IDEAS

This lesson plan revolves around the story of *Maya the Clothes Maker and Ramon, the Button Maker* (find out more at www.mathxplorers.org).

The story presents simulated real-world problems, connecting students' interests and identification with the characters to an empathetic desire to help them overcome challenges. This approach builds on children's existing knowledge of the world. By integrating simulated real-world problems, children are encouraged to explore, analyze, and develop their problem-solving strategies. They then connect the math ideas into conceptual and logical reasoning through context-driven and open-ended problem-solving.

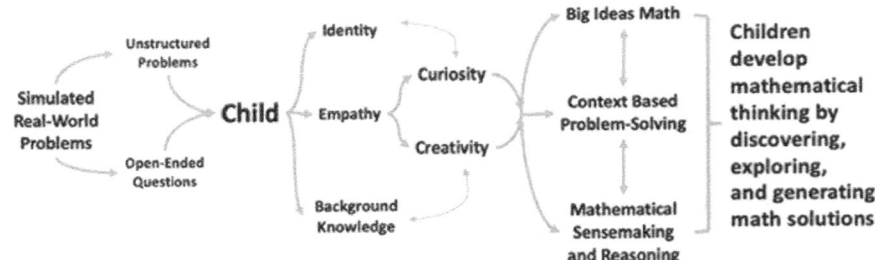

To foster an *equal playing field*, these lessons provide students with a review of *foundational math concepts*. The lessons focus on *conceptual learning through mathematical modeling, sensemaking,* and the steps to achieve these goals. In the publication *Becoming a Teacher of Mathematical Modeling,* the National Council of Teachers of Mathematics (Arnold et al., 2021) describes mathematical modeling:

1. Modeling begins and ends outside the mathematical world.
2. Modeling deals with solutions that are open and complex.
3. Modelers exercise judgment when investigating problems. These judgments stem from a set of numerical values that may or may not be fully articulated but are always present.
4. Modelers decide when a solution is good enough.

RELATED INSTRUCTIONAL AREAS

Although the story focuses primarily on mathematics, it also offers opportunities for companion instruction on the following topics:

- English language arts (ELA)
- Social and emotional learning (SEL)
- Design and engineering

English Language Arts (ELA)

This methodology deliberately integrates storytelling into mathematics learning, enabling the teacher to include English language instruction. ***Open-ended questions*** throughout the story *create opportunities to enhance awareness of characters and plot, practice integrating and articulating relevant aspects of prior knowledge*, and *understand and observe the story elements and mathematics challenges*.

Social and Emotional Learning (SEL)

The story engages children by introducing relatable characters and encouraging them to assist community members in solving their problems. SEL opportunities may include prompting children to reflect on times when they have helped someone in their family or neighborhood or to envision situations where they could offer support.

STEM/STEAM

Integrating mathematical concepts into simulated real-world scenarios enhances student engagement, fostering active participation and deeper understanding. Incorporating elements of science, technology, engineering, arts, and design into math-related stories and challenges broadens learning experiences, allowing children to grasp diverse concepts and problem-solving strategies while developing their mathematical skills. Applying mathematical concepts to simulated real-world situations makes math problems more engaging for students, leading to greater involvement and improved overall learning outcomes. The math stories and challenges can incorporate science, technology, engineering, arts, and design. By doing so, children learn various ideas and processes in multiple subjects as they learn math.

**Personalized Approach to
Conceptual Mathematical Understanding**

OVERVIEW OF THE STORY

Maya and Ramon live in the *Town of Whatever*. The people from the town lacked confidence in using math to solve problems. They are joined by their friend Bikoy, who loves math and works with them to address the urgent issue of completing a unique shirt for a very tall man.

In this story, children discover algebraic thinking by adding to, putting together, and using the equal and unequal signs to represent a numeric answer. The story weaves together the following math concepts or *Big Ideas*.

There are many ways to extend the story into more advanced lessons.

As students grow in their understanding of math ideas and applications to problem-solving simulated real-world situations and challenges, you can elevate the challenges accordingly:

1. Connect addition to subtraction and multiplication with the challenges.
2. Adjust the numbers in the challenges to fit the mathematical levels of your students and classes.

You know your students and children best. Adjust as needed. Extend the story as you raise the levels of the challenges.

STRUCTURE OF THE STORY

The story and the lessons are divided into three parts.

Part 1: Introduction

The *Town of Whatever* and the story characters are introduced.

Activity 1: Sets of Buttons

Objectives:

- Identify and articulate the problem (organizing buttons)
- Identify different parameters of categorization

Math Activities:

- Build the 3D button box
- Color and sort buttons by type
- Record totals on the button map

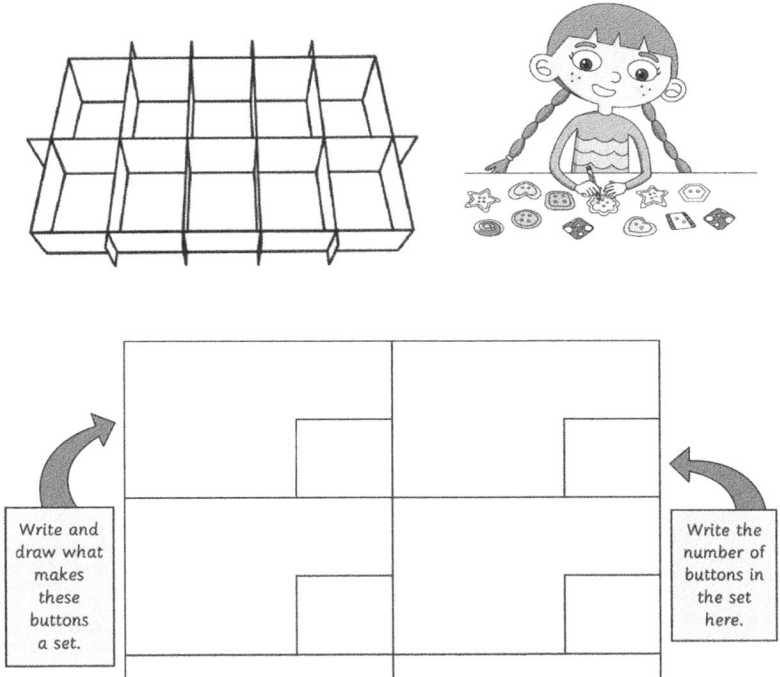

Part 2: Exploration

The *Town of Whatever* and the story characters are introduced.

Activity 2: Solve for Missing Buttons

Objectives:

- Develop designs that reflect equations and conceptual transfer of *visual number patterns* and *equations*
- Learn how *bigger* numbers can be made from *smaller* numbers
- Observe that there are *different ways to build numbers*

$$10 = 5 + 5$$

$$10 = 2 + 8$$

Math Activities:

- Identify and add numbers from the faces of dice
- Write equations as part of the t-shirt design process

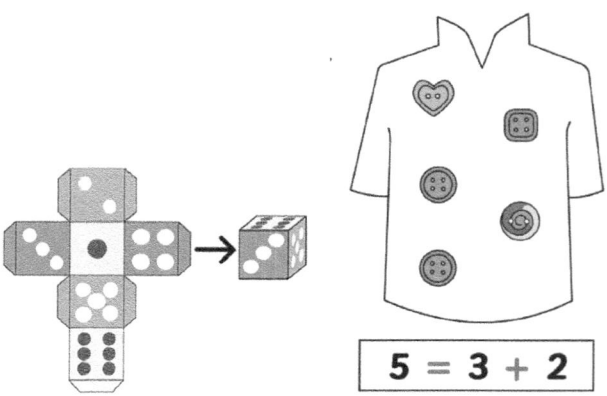

$$5 = 3 + 2$$

Part 3: Design

Story ending

Activity 3: Button Festival

Objectives:

- Identify patterns in number sequences
- Show how ascending and descending sequences relate to addition to a common total
- Discuss how the repetition of elements creates a pattern

Math Activities:

- Complete number patterns to reveal a code
- Design button patterns for the Button Festival

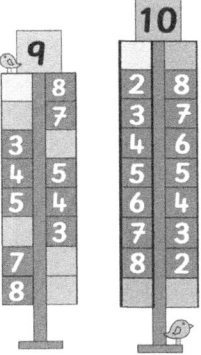

ELEMENTS OF THE LESSON

Open-Ended Questions

The lesson activities in the book aim to be interactive and spark conversations. Some pages in the story feature green-boxed questions with discussion prompts or open-ended inquiries that help you explore each student's interests and evaluate their attitudes and beliefs about math.

Students' ideas are valued. Encourage each child to share ideas related to the question based on their knowledge and experiences. Use a "turn and talk" strategy to allow all students to speak. To encourage dialogue, you can post and use response prompts like,

- "I agree/disagree with (idea, not person) because _____."
  or
- "Something I'm confused about is _____."

By design, the open-ended questions in this book:

- Encourage children to share their ideas and invite diverse perspectives.
- There is more than one correct answer, which cannot be answered with yes or no. (Answers may also contain opinions and feelings.)
- Highlight children's insights and inspire students to think and reflect.
- Invite acceptance of all ideas.
- Cultivate a *dynamic* learning experience and *open minds* by encouraging flexible thinking that naturally allows for differentiation. This means evolving solutions and interactions that build on students' contributions and palpable energy and excitement among the learners.
- Invite student responses that offer deeper insights into their interests and mathematical comprehension. When students sense that teachers care about what is significant to them, they feel more connected and safer, which encourages them to persist in exploring and testing solutions.
- Create an environment where students teach and learn from each other, acting as active participants rather than passive listeners, with the teacher as a facilitator.

Note: Children may initially need clarification on open-ended questions, particularly if they have not been exposed to this type of discussion.

The image exemplifies a 1st-grade student's response to the open-ended question, *How many ways can we get to 10? How can we write our math ideas in the form of equations?*

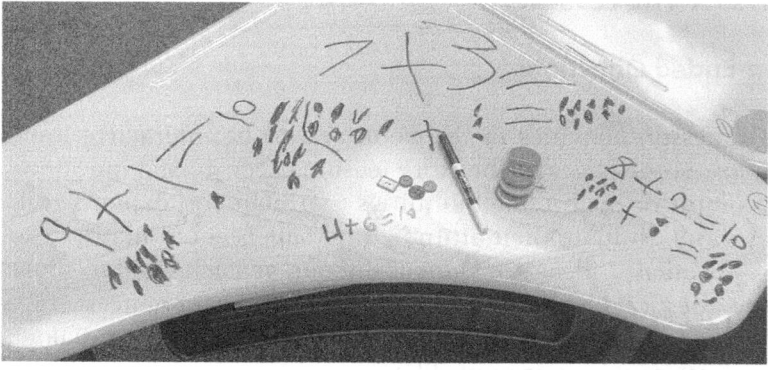

Common Core Connections

The mathematics in this story is aligned with Common Core milestones developed by the National Council of Teachers of Mathematics (NCTM; Table 5.1).

Table 5.1. Big Ideas Are Linked to State Benchmarks

Big Idea or Activity	Common Core Mathematical Standard
Sets are groups of the same types of objects.	**Kindergarten Counting and Cardinality (K.CC)** **Kindergarten Measurement & Data (K.MD)** —Describe and compare measurable attributes, classify objects, and count the number of objects in each category.
Numbers tell how many.	**Kindergarten Counting and Cardinality (K.CC)** —Know number names and the count sequence, count to tell the number of objects, compare numbers.
Equal means the same.	**1st-Grade Operations and Algebraic Thinking (1.OA-7)** —Work with addition and subtraction equations.
There are many ways to take numbers apart. Smaller numbers make bigger numbers.	**1st-Grade Operations and Algebraic Thinking (1.OA.1–8)** —Represent and solve problems involving addition and subtraction, understand and apply properties of operations and the relationship between addition and subtraction, add and subtract within 20, work with addition and subtraction equations.
A pattern is a repeating order of objects.	**1st-Grade Geometry (1.G)** —Reason with shapes and their attributes.
Activity 1: Button Sort	**Kindergarten Counting and Cardinality (K.CC)** **Kindergarten Measurement & Data (K.MD)** **1st-Grade Geometry (1.G)**
Activity 2: Shirt Design	**1.OA.1–8 Operations and Algebraic Thinking** **1st-Grade Geometry (1.G)**
Activity 3: The Button Festival	**1.OA.1–8 Operations and Algebraic Thinking** **1st-Grade Geometry (1.G)**

Mathematical Practices

The Common Core also lists several *Standards for Mathematical Practices*, which describe ways students should interact with mathematical content. These practices provide children with opportunities to develop their comfort and skill in approaching and applying math ideas across all areas of math.

Students will learn by:

- Reasoning abstractly and quantitatively,
- Modeling with mathematics,
- Using appropriate tools strategically,
- Attending to precision, and
- Looking for and expressing regularity in repeated reasoning.

Math stories empower children to discover, explore, and create mathematical solutions. Narratives and images provide scenarios and clues to connect with and understand the content, reason through it, think creatively, and begin to shape their identities as capable young mathematicians. With encouragement and a safe, intercultural classroom environment, these practices evolve and mature over many years alongside a student's mathematical learning journey.

Maya the Clothes Maker and Ramon the Button Maker provide developmentally appropriate opportunities for children 5–7 years old to explore mathematical sensemaking and reasoning by focusing on the following three mathematical practices.

1. Make Sense of Problems and Persevere in Solving Them

Questions guide students in making sense of problems and figuring out solutions. The following questions are formulated to assure students that their unique perspectives matter and that there is no one correct answer. Removing the anxiety of giving the "wrong" answer will result in greater engagement and understanding.

Examples of Questions to Ask Students:

- What do you think is the problem?
- Based on what you observe and know from the story and illustrations, what is causing the problem?
- What mathematical idea(s) do you observe that can help you understand the problem?
- How can the problem be solved? Could you write or draw your solution?

Student Objectives:

- Explain the meaning of the problem and look for entry points to finding a solution.

- Understand more than one solution path.
- Check answers and continually ask, "Does this make sense?"

Examples From the Story: Maya and Ramon model perseverance when determining how many buttons they need, only to realize they do not have enough. Together with Bikoy, they investigate and find a creative solution with *patterns*. This leads to a conceptual understanding of the *commutative property* because switching the order of the button sets does not change the total amount.

2. Construct Viable Arguments

Guide students to explain their thinking. Tell students that in math, *arguments* mean multiple *explanations*. A sentence structure with prompts can guide the *explanations*.

> *Question*: What do you think is the problem?
> *Answer Prompt*: *I think the problem is* (state the problem).
> *Question*: Based on what you observe and know from the story and illustrations, what is causing the problem?
> *Answer Prompt*: *From what I observe* (describe what you see in the illustrations) and *what I know* (say what you know from the story), *what is causing the problem is* (explain your idea about the problem).
> *Question*: What mathematical idea(s) do you observe that can help you understand the problem?
> *Answer Prompt*: *From what I observe, the big idea(s) that can help us understand the problem is/are* (show and read the Big Idea cards and then explain why these are related to the problem).
> *Question*: How can the problem be solved? Write and draw your way. There is always more than one way.
> *Answer Prompt*: *The problem can be solved by* (explain your solution).

Student Objectives:

- Understand and use assumptions, vocabulary, and prior knowledge to explain ideas and make conjectures using objects, drawings, diagrams, and actions.
- Analyze situations, give examples, and recognize counterexamples.
- Learn from the reasoning of peers, focus on ideas rather than personalities, and respond accordingly.

"Each of your patterns are made of sets. Each set has a total number of buttons." Bikoy explains about equations and buttons. "You will know the total number of buttons for each pattern when you write an equation.

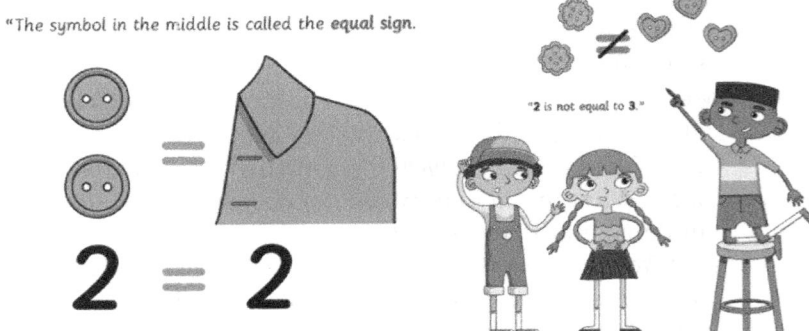

Examples From the Story: Bikoy explains the concept of *equality* to Maya and Ramon with buttons. He explains there must be the same number of buttons as buttonholes and gives a visual counterexample when he shows that 2 is *not* equal to 3.

"The symbol in the middle is called the **equal sign**.

"2 is not equal to 3."

2 = 2

Maya critiques Ramon's reasoning when she states, "But then the top buttons won't be the same color and shape as the bottom ones."

But then the top buttons won't be the same color and shape as the bottom ones.

Maya is not sure about mixing buttons on the same shirt.

3. Look For and Make Use of Structure

Guide students to look closely to find a pattern or structure.

Student Objectives:

- Understand the role of repetition in defining patterns.
- Notice that repetition and sequence can exist along multiple axes for any set of objects.

Examples From the Book—The Button Festival:

- Notice geometric structures as they analyze individual shapes.
- Analyze pattern structure as they identify the pattern's repeating part (term).
- Notice and annotate patterns with letters, such as *ABAB* or *ABBCABBC*.

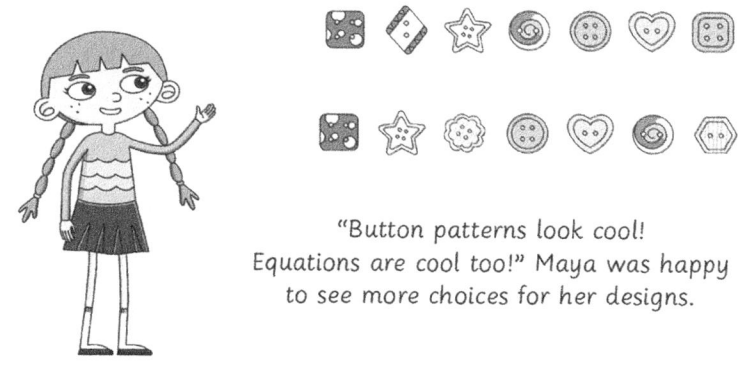

"Button patterns look cool!
Equations are cool too!" Maya was happy
to see more choices for her designs.

The Number Signs on the Way to the Button Festival:

- Find structure in the number system of the signs on the way to the Button Festival. For example, children may notice sequencing structure: The numbers on the left side are in ascending order (get bigger), while on the right side, they are in descending order (get smaller), and each time the numbers change by 1.
- Discover the part–part–whole structure or the pairs of numbers remaining unchanged although their order changes.

FEEDBACK, SHARING STUDENT WORKS, AND ASSESSMENT (PORTFOLIO)

Students perform best when they receive immediate *feedback*, which you can provide as you monitor students and take notes. Make sure students know that mistakes are among the most valuable learning experiences because the challenge to find what went wrong makes your brain grow more than when something is easy.

Having students *share* their work with the class and display it in the classroom provides opportunities for feedback, reflection, and pride in their work. Guide students on how to give feedback in the form of a compliment, notice, or question.

After finishing *Maya and Ramon,* you may collect student work or take pictures of it for inclusion in their *portfolios.*

ELEVATING STORY EQUATIONS TO ALGEBRAIC THINKING

EXPERIENCE

Algebraic Thinking: Objects and Pieces

Materials:

- Object cut-outs
- Plus, the letter X, equal signs

Steps:

1. Place two objects side by side. Ask the children, *Are these two objects the same?*

 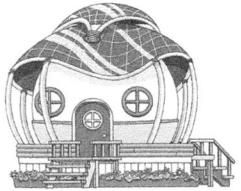

Encourage the children to analyze closely.
When they all agree that the objects are the same, then say,
"In math, equal means the same."
Then, add the equal sign between the objects.

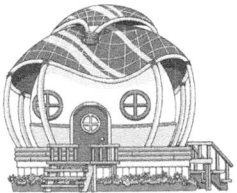 =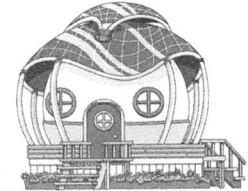

In math, this is called an equation. Engage children in a conversation about the parts of an equation. An **equation** is a **mathematical statement** that shows the equality between two expressions. It contains **numbers, variables, and mathematical operations**, always including an **equal sign (=),** indicating that both sides are the same.

---

2. Take apart one of the objects. Ask the children, *Are these objects the same?* Encourage different views.

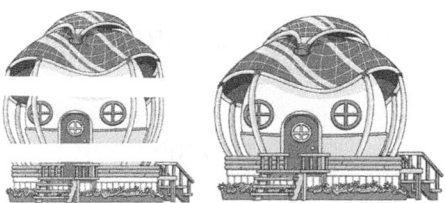

3. In math, the plus sign means these parts are connected.

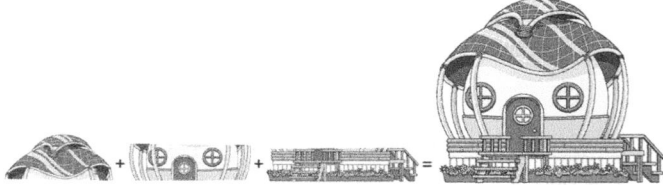

4. What happens when I remove one object? It is missing, and we don't know what the object is. Remind the children about the game *Hot and Cold*. Then, ask, *What did we call the missing object?* Acknowledge the use of *X* as a *mathematical symbol* of the missing object.

Do the same with the pieces of the object. The goal is for children to understand that **X** symbolizes a missing object of an equation.

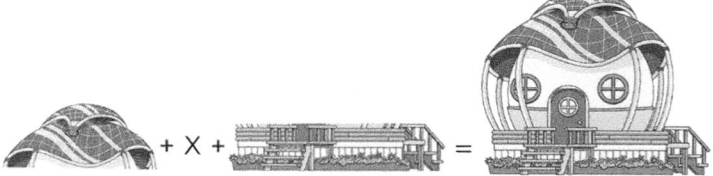

5. Let's do equations with squares. How many ways can we make 10?

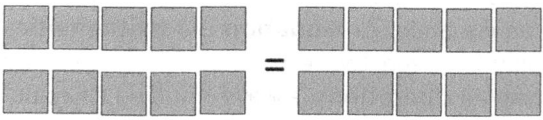

6. When the children are ready, the conversation about equations and building numbers can extend to using number symbols. For example:

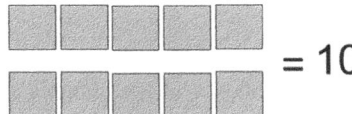

7. Connect the problems in the story with simple algebraic equations using *X* for the missing number.

Background Notes:

Algebraic thinking is fundamental to mathematical thinking because it involves *recognizing patterns*, *understanding relationships*, and using *logical reasoning* to solve problems. Mathematics, at its core, is about *making sense of numbers*, *structures*, and *relationships*, and algebraic thinking provides a *structured way* to approach these ideas. Algebraic thinking is a key part of mathematical thinking because it allows us to *analyze*, *generalize*, and *solve problems systematically*. It serves as the bridge between arithmetic (basic calculations) and higher-level mathematics (functions, calculus, etc.), making it an essential skill for mathematical reasoning.

Connections Between Algebraic Thinking and Mathematical Thinking

Patterns and Relationships	
Mathematical thinking involves identifying how numbers and operations interact.	Algebraic thinking helps us generalize these relationships into equations and functions.
Example: Noticing that in the sequence 3, 6, 9, 12, each number increases by 3 (a mathematical pattern) can be expressed algebraically as $y = 3x$.	
Abstract and Symbolic Representation	
Mathematics often moves beyond specific numbers to abstract symbols and general rules.	Algebraic thinking allows us to use variables and symbols to represent unknowns and relationships.
Example: Instead of saying "if I add 5 to a number, I get 12," algebra expresses it as $x + 5 = 12$.	
Logical Reasoning and Problem Solving	
Mathematical thinking involves making sense of problems and finding solutions logically.	Algebraic thinking helps us set up equations, test solutions, and verify answers.
Example: A word problem like "Ramon has twice as many buttons as Maya. Together, they have 12 buttons. How many does each have?"	
Algebra helps express it as $R = 2M$ and $R + M = 12$, making it solvable.	

(continued)

Generalization and Making Connections

Mathematical thinking often seeks general principles that apply to different situations.	Algebraic thinking allows us to extend rules and patterns to broader contexts.

Example: Recognizing that the distributive property $a(b+c) = ab + ac$ applies not just to numbers but also to real-world applications like area calculations.

Problem Representation and Modeling

Mathematical thinking often requires representing real-world problems mathematically.	Algebraic thinking helps translate complex situations into mathematical models.

Example: Understanding linear relationships, such as how the amount of time to make buttons change with how much buttons can be produced, can be modeled using algebraic equations.

Where:

- N = Number of buttons produced
- T = Time spent making buttons (e.g., in minutes or hours)
- R = Production Rate (buttons per unit of time)

Using the Model to Make Predictions: $N = RT$

A worker can produce 5 buttons per minute

How many buttons can be made in 10 minutes?

$B = 5(10) = 50$

In **10 minutes, 50 buttons** can be produced.

Reflect:

- How does the lesson introduce algebraic thinking?

Connected and Contextualized Learning Through Math Stories:

The lesson activities integrate Vygotsky's well-known concept of the zone of proximal development. The intersections of natural language through fictional narrative, mathematical ideas, open-ended questions, and images bridge the gap between a child's current developmental level—determined by their ability to solve problems independently—and their potential developmental level, which can be attained with assistance from an adult or more skilled peers during problem-solving activities.

Children learn about the missing X as a vital part of mathematical problem-solving. As they begin to think in equations, they progress from concrete to abstract concepts and from play to mathematical modeling.

The math story and lesson activities nurture higher-order thinking. Children observe, reflect, make connections, and learn new ideas from their classmates' contributions and perspectives. Students discover, develop, and value their observations and analytical skills. The process acknowledges the learner as a resource for shaping knowledge. Mathematician Alan Schoenfeld (2014) explains:

> Effective teaching calls for understanding and building upon what students bring—their predispositions, habits of mind, patterns of engagement, patterns of communication (including norms of social interaction and linguistic patterns), and more. . . . Many of these are shaped by the students' experiences outside classroom boundaries—that is, they are shaped culturally. (p. 6)

Lessons from math stories engage the child as a human being and mathematics as an element of being human. The connections shaped by the intersections of natural language, visual images, and mathematical ideas are concrete and abstract and connect on both cognitive and emotional levels.

CHAPTER 6

Teachers as Math Storytellers

EXPERIENCE

Storytelling Is Teaching

Storytelling is a skill you already use in your classroom! Let's tap into your storytelling experiences to build connections between your strengths and math teaching.

Steps:

1. Reflect on when you told/read a story in class. This could be during circle time, a read-aloud, or when you used storytelling to introduce or teach a new concept.
2. What were the memorable moments of storytelling with your students?
3. Let's authenticate storytelling theories based on your experiences. Write highlights in a mind map about:
   - Emotional connections to the story
   - Children's connections to the ideas of the story
4. Utilize a mind map to underscore critical storytelling elements and children's reactions to create a framework for teaching with stories.

Here is an example:

> Reflect:
>
> - What is it about stories that children love?
> - How do their reactions inform teachers about stories being powerful tools for engagement and learning?
>
> This chapter will discuss how storytelling techniques used in story circles can be used to teach math. We will build upon your storytelling strengths and intersect mathematical ideas, vocabulary, and processes to transform the math classroom into an engaged community of learners.

MATH STORYTELLERS GUIDE MATHEMATICAL THINKING

Storytelling elements and techniques generate opportunities for meaningful math learning. Students develop a deeper understanding of mathematical concepts and how to apply them to solve problems. These goals inspire learning through stories while building children's abilities to utilize mathematical skills and ideas in various contexts.

- *Conceptual understanding*
  Understand the "why" behind the math rather than just memorizing formulas and procedures.
- *Real-world applications*
  Explore how math is used in everyday life, such as determining how much to tip at a restaurant.
- *Teamwork*
  Achieve productive peer interaction through collaboration and communication.
- *Analytical thinking*
  Elevate skills with conceptual mathematical thinking to solve complex problems.

INSPIRE CHILDREN TO FIGURE OUT POSSIBILITIES

Teaching through storytelling will require children to participate in story adventures. Their engagement with mathematical ideas and problem-solving will propel the narrative forward. Learners will problem-solve, do hands-on activities, and play math games related to the stories.

Math learning is intercultural in a multicultural environment with children of different cultures. This requires considering vocabulary, images, situations, and characters from multicultural perspectives. Children will intersect each other's cultural lenses and develop intercultural competencies. Open-mindedness to one and the other's ideas makes it possible to build better solutions. Moreover, math learning integrates universal math ideas with cross-cultural values.

Embedded math ideas guide conceptual understanding and applications. While reading the story, they figure out solutions and learn mathematical expressions. With math feeling more like interacting with an adventure story, children learn by exploring multiple possibilities without fear of making mistakes. Like young mathematicians, young learners will make mathematical sense of situations and problems. They will know the relational values of mathematical ideas and processes and how these can be applied to varied contexts. Children develop confidence in their mathematical abilities and enjoy math learning. Their productive and meaningful experiences increase mathematical proficiency, confidence, and agency.

As a storyteller, you will tap into stories that offer webs of connections, using nuanced approaches that touch upon emotions, cultural values, and new ideas. With math stories, storytelling makes math real, interspersed with children's natural language and everyday life experiences.

SAMPLE 30-MINUTE LESSON STRATEGIES

Children Will Explore These Math Ideas

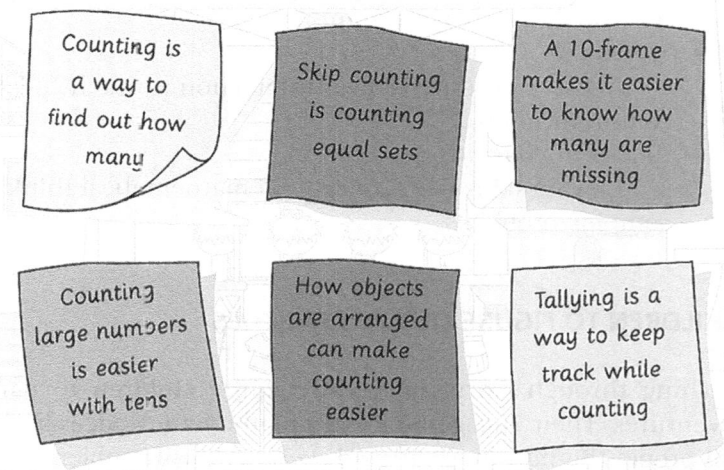

Lesson 1: Counting Large Numbers

Read the Text for Context:

Misha and Iliana are taking the train from the city to the Town of Whatever. "Let's play a game and see how many power poles we can count!," says Misha. Iliana counts, "1 pole, 2 poles," then, "3, 4, 5, 6, 7, 8, 9, 10 poles." She takes a big breath. "The train is going too fast! I need a better way to count."

Ask a question: What are some ways Iliana can count faster?

Provide clues: What do you see? Why does Iliana need to count faster?

Guide observation: Guide students using visual indicators and parameters to engage children in counting by 5s:

- Look for visual patterns in the illustration.
- Notice the arrangement of the power poles.
- Count how many poles fit into a window.
- Encourage children to double-check each other's responses.

Ask a purpose question: Why does Iliana have to count faster?

Connect children's responses: Weave observations and insights into math concepts.

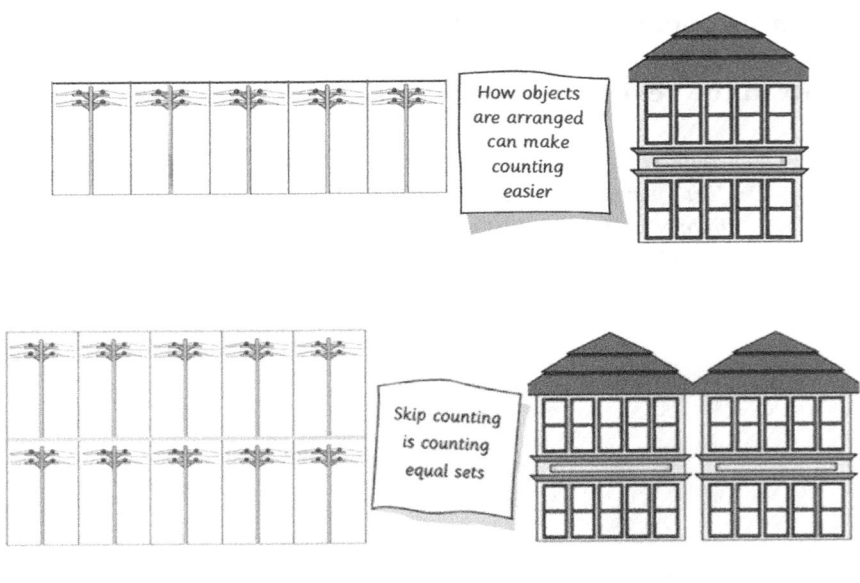

5, 10, 15 . . .   **10, 20, 30 . . .**

Review math ideas: Involve children in visualizing math ideas in varied ways.

Differentiate: Instruct advanced students to create and share advanced applications of skip counting, sets, and patterns and share these with their peers. Provide a few clues to elevate their levels of mathematical abilities.

Lesson 2: Skip Counting

Start with rhythm: Use a percussion instrument to sound the beats. Count 1 to 10 with the children.

Read the Text for Context:

> *At last, Misha and Iliana arrive at the market where they hear drums.*
> *Iliana claps her hands to the beat and counts, "1." She snaps her fingers and counts, "2."*
> *Iliana claps, "3," and snaps, "4." She continues to do the same with 5, 6, 7, 8, 9, 10.*

Engage with rhythm and movement: Use percussion sounds as beats. Count 1 to 10. Add movements guided by the text.

Engage with rhythm, movement, and poetry: Use percussion sound beats. Instruct students to repeat every phrase you recite.

In the market, people dance,
Shaking legs, arms, and hands!

1, 2, next is 3,
Count by ones, you then me!

2, 4, then it's 6,
Count by 2s, let's do skips!

Skip counting means adding the same number each time to the previous number. It is repeated addition, which is the basis of multiplication. Skip counting is important in developing fluency in calculation and number sense and supports the basis of multiplication and division.

Math is the science of patterns. Skip counting is the practice of counting numbers in patterns. Equal groups of numbers are added to the previous number, building a progressive pattern of increasing number sets. Awareness of number patterns develops prediction abilities with same-pattern numbers. In 2s, the following number is two more. In 5s, five more, and 10s, ten more. In the 3rd and 4th grades, students advance to skip counting more numbers. This is helpful in mastering multiplication facts.

1, 2, 3-4-5
Jump and clap, we're so alive!

6, 7, 8-9-10
Turn around, now do it again!

6, 7, 8-9-10
We did it once, we did it again!

REFRAIN:

Stomp by ones, 1 to 10!
Clap by twos, 2 to 20!

Stomp by fives, 5 to 50!
Clap by tens to 100!

Practice through repetition: Repeat each of the skip-counting numbers. Use percussion sound beats to keep the children in step.

Build understanding through creative movement: Divide the class into groups. Have them create dance moves for each of the skip counting sets. Encourage students to practice their dance steps.

REFRAIN:

Shake your bones 1 to 10
Stomp the rhythm 2 to 20

Shake your bones 5 to 50
Stomp ten to one hundred!

Review skip counting: Read the above text and instruct students to repeat after each line. In the refrain, each group performs their part.

Rhythm and rhyme with sound beats are intuitive approaches to learning skip counting. When applied to counting, skip counting feels like a joyous, rhythmic beat of numbers—like reciting words in a poem.

Lesson 3: Ruby's Ice Cream Truck

Read the Text for Context:

Iliana walks over to Ruby's ice cream truck. She chooses her two favorite flavors.
"I would like one scoop of Merry Cherry and one scoop of Choco Loco, please."

While she waits, Iliana counts the children.
She stomps her left foot, "1," then right foot, "2."
She continues, "3, 4, 5, 6, 7, 8, 9, 10 children
lining up for Ruby's Ice Cream!"

Instruct Students to Count: How many children are there?

Next, she counts the cones in the rack,
"1, 2, 3, 4, 5, 6, 7, 8, 9.

Oh no, 9 cones for 10 kids!"

Ice Cream Cone Rack Counting Tool: How did Iliana know there were only 9 cones?

Relate Counting to Addition and Subtraction: How many holes does the rack have?

Correlate the Number of Holes With the Number of Cones: How many cones are there?

Extend to Addition and Subtraction: How did you know?

Learning is an active process in which students construct new ideas based on their knowledge. By allowing children to invent their own math stories or strategies, students actively construct their knowledge, experiment with different solutions, and build understanding through experience.

The lesson demonstrates how to prepare children to successfully intersect their natural abilities and prior knowledge with new math ideas. This strategy is called *scaffolding*. The activities integrate breaking down concepts into smaller pieces and presenting them in multiple ways, guiding students to make sense cumulatively and relationally.

These series of activities interweave counting, addition, and subtraction and offer open-ended opportunities for problem-solving. The cone rack functions as a real-world math tool for understanding the one-to-one correspondence of numbers with cones and holes.

In a conceptual learning pedagogy, children use prior knowledge and experiences to learn math ideas that grow their comprehension of how numbers are formed and how they can be decomposed. With a teacher asking guiding questions and providing clues students learn best when working within what Lev Vygotsky calls the zone of proximal development. Teachers should offer just enough support to help students reach the next level of understanding.

EXPERIENCE

Zone of Proximal Development (ZPD)

In this part of the story, the narrative highlights Ruby, the ice cream maker's, prior knowledge of skip counting. How does the story raise the mathematical understanding of children with a range of mathematical ability levels and diverse backgrounds

"I love **skip counting by 10s!**"
Ruby dances as she
counts her cones,
"**10, 20, 30, 40, 50!**"

How can Ruby use the racks to count the ice cream cones she sells?

Prepare for your next lesson by grouping the students according to three levels of mathematical ability. Use the story's text to create three challenges that elevate each group's capabilities. Help Ruby by using the cone racks as a math tool for counting, addition, and subtraction.

Read the following text as an example of how the cone rack works:

Iliana has an idea! "Look, each time you sell a cone,
it leaves another empty hole. When you see **1** hole,
it means **9** cones are left, because **9** plus **1** equals **10**.
When you see **2** holes..."

"I have **8** cones left," sings Ruby.

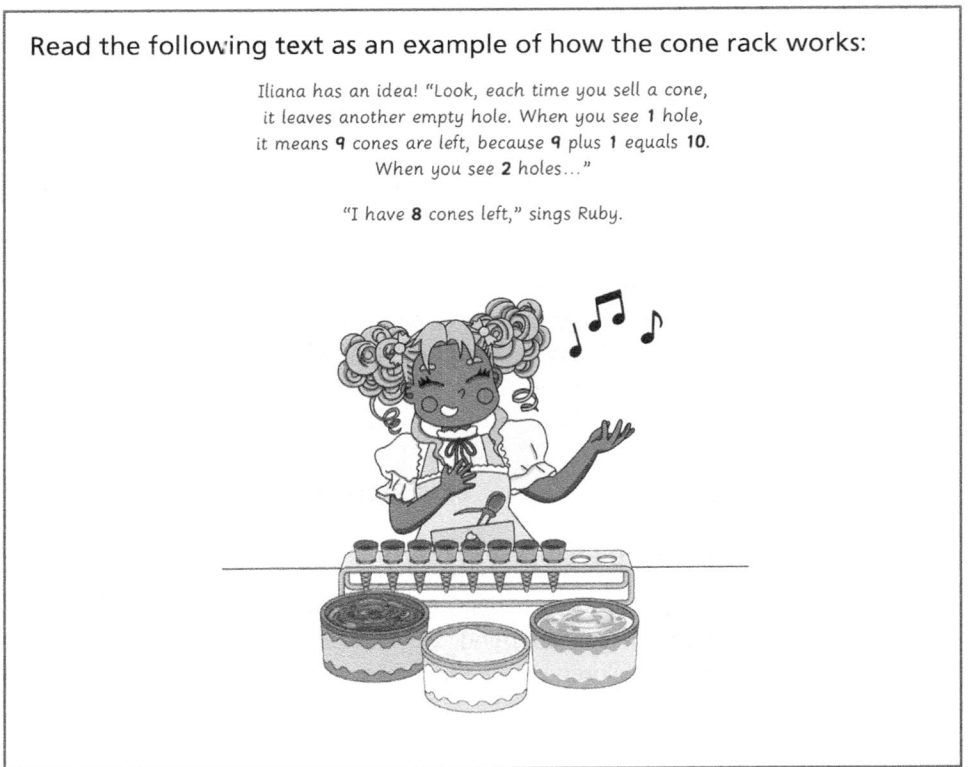

Lesson 4: Mathematical Modeling

Jiménez and Verschaffel (2014) examined how children develop solutions to nonstandard arithmetic word problems. The authors explain that *standard problems are clearly and undoubtedly modeled by applying one or a combination of the four basic arithmetic operations with the numbers provided in the problem.* These beliefs include the assumptions that (1) every word problem is solvable, (2) there is only one correct numerical answer, (3) calculations are always necessary, and (4) all numbers provided must be used to find the solution. However, *not all word and mathematical problems are solvable.* Learning math using a limited understanding of word problems creates a mindset that one is not mathematically able when failing to solve a problem. The authors emphasized exposing students to various problems to foster analytical and flexible thinking and problem-solving skills.

Freudenthal's educational philosophy views mathematics as a human activity connected to everyday life. As the creator of realistic mathematics education (RME), he emphasized the importance of using real-world scenarios to help students understand mathematical concepts, tools, and procedures.

Sample scenarios that are relatable and meaningful to the student originate from real life, fairy tales, or formal mathematics. The principles of RME inspire the stories and illustrations found in MathXplorers' picture books (Freudenthal, 1973). Also dubbed as *mathematizing*, which means modeling a context in mathematical terms, RME promotes mathematical thinking through modeling, building on students' natural sensemaking with familiar contexts.

Studies have been conducted on RME, demonstrating how it enriches mathematics education. Yuanita et al. (2018) examined the effectiveness of the RME approach, focusing on the role of mathematical representation as a mediator between mathematical beliefs and problem-solving skills. RME increases mathematical understanding, for instance, representation, and problem-solving skills. This approach successfully trains students to formulate their ideas from real-life situations or experiences. The Wisconsin Center for Education Research (2005) published an in-depth *Longitudinal/Cross-Sectional Study of the Impact of Teaching Mathematics Using Mathematics in Context on Student Achievement*. This research provided an in-depth analysis of student performance between those taught using the Mathematics in Context curriculum and those receiving conventional mathematics instruction. Students using the context-based curriculum demonstrated a deeper understanding of mathematical concepts and improved problem-solving skills. The study highlights the effectiveness of context in promoting a comprehensive mathematical education that balances conceptual knowledge with essential computational abilities.

Through mathematical modeling, students learn to look for and discuss relationships among mathematical ideas, express an understanding of mathematical topics, or explain their solution strategies for relatively complex problems in which two or more mathematical ideas are integrated (Newmann et al., 1995). Shafer (2004) emphasizes how students learn mathematics with understanding when these connections are promoted.

When connections are drawn between and among mathematical ideas, students can link procedural and conceptual knowledge, recognize relationships between representations, and recognize the interconnectedness of mathematical topics (NCTM, 1989).

This lesson provides RME applications and includes the process that emphasizes gradually formalizing math models, supported by interactive teaching in whole-class settings.

In this lesson, the class will engage in:

- **Informal sensemaking:** RME starts with students' intuitive understanding of meaningful situations.
- **Progressive formalization:** It transitions from informal ideas to formal math models.
- **Interactive teaching:** RME uses active, interactive teaching methods.

- **Active student engagement:** Encourages participation through discussions and Q&A sessions.
- **Connecting concepts:** RME helps students link different mathematical ideas.

This is your class. As such, you will have a unique interpretation of the RME process.

Read the Text for Context:

Farmer Antonio explains, "The boxes make it easier for me to count and organize the fruits. It's easier to see how many fruits I'm selling when they are in my special boxes."

Can you tell how many fruits there are in each of the boxes without counting?

Subitizing is "seeing" the number.

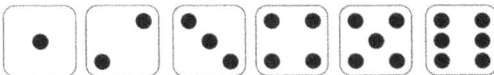

Subitizing is the ability to instantly recognize a small number of objects without counting them individually. On the other hand, counting involves systematically going through each item to determine the total number. Subitizing is seeing the number; when you subitize, you essentially "just know" how many objects there are by quickly glancing at them, often based on patterns or familiar arrangements. A familiar experience in subitizing is when we play a game using dice. We know the number by seeing the way the dots are organized.

> *The word subitizing comes from the Latin word "subitis," which means "sudden." Subitizing is a cognitive process that allows our brain to see a small quantity of objects quickly or suddenly and know how many there are without counting one by one.* (Hagan-Howe, 2024)

In the preceding image, subitizing is used to recognize numbers in groups of objects. It is also a springboard to addition and subtraction, using patterns of objects as pictorial renditions of numbers. Contextualized in a real-world math problem, the narrative's goal is for children to tap into and grow their subitizing and pattern-recognition abilities in problem-solving.

Read the Text for Context:

> *"When I have lots of customers, I need to count fast.*
> *Look at this square box, it has **4** pomegranates.*
> *If someone orders **12** pieces, I can easily **Skip count by 4s**."*

Pose an open-ended calculation problem: How many of each box above would Farmer Antonio need for 20 of each fruit?

Inform children that they will be creating mathematical models of their solutions. In the case of Farmer Antonio, who cannot write number symbols, the idea of tallying is introduced. The term *tally* originates from the Latin word *talea*, meaning "twig" or "cutting" (Harper, 2024). Tally marks are a way to record a number of objects and keep track of counting in groups of five. They are also a simple visual version of skip counting by 5s.

"What if you use a **tally**?" asks Misha. He takes a piece of chalk from his pocket and draws lines side by side. "Tallying can help you keep track of your fruits."

The following examples are forms of mathematical modeling with concrete and abstract representations. You can support children in modeling their equations with various strategies.

Informal sensemaking: For every child's thinking to surface in the early modeling discussions.

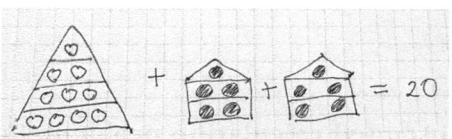

Progressive formalization: Ask leveling-up questions:

- How many ways can we get to 20?
- How many 4s, 5s, and 10s are there in 20?

Conceptual understanding: Conceptual mathematical thinking is the ability to understand the relationships between mathematical ideas, patterns, and procedures and to apply that understanding to new problems. It is a deeper level of knowledge than procedural fluency, which is the ability to follow the steps of a mathematical equation.

Conceptual mathematical thinking also involves elevating thought processes. Students engage in metacognition by reflecting on their thinking. Rather than concentrating solely on correct answers, open-ended questions about the process encourage students to contemplate their learning journey and the reasoning behind their solutions, fostering a deeper understanding of how one learns and thinks, in this case, mathematically.

TEACHING TIPS IN MATH STORYTELLING

Generate opportunities for meaningful math applications:

1. **Model math ideas, operations, and strategies in context.**
   - Model/act out math concepts with props and visuals, for example, grouping objects to solve problems
2. **Ask guiding questions** to promote critical thinking and exploration.
   - *Are there objects in the scene that the character could use to solve the problem?*
   - *How would grouping the apples help the character count?*
3. **Provide clues** to scaffold learning.
   - In a measurement story, the teacher can say, *The character has a string that's 3 feet long. How many strings would they need to cover the entire path?*
4. **Encourage with guiding prompts** to serve as clues.
   - *You're getting close—keep thinking about what the character did. What's the next step they might take?*
   - Reinforce that mistakes are part of the learning process.
5. **Provide space and time** for exploration.
   - Encourage children to invent their math strategies. *Can you try doing something similar? Can you try doing something different? What other shapes or groupings could you try?*

- Have students articulate and/or write their responses by expanding the math story in various directions based on their mathematical insights.

6. **Facilitate social interaction and collaborative group work** to encourage intercultural collective math meaning-making.
   - *Can you collaborate with your partner to solve this? Let's think about it as a group: how would we solve this challenge differently?*
   - Focusing on the thought processes rather than the correct answers diminishes math anxiety.
   - *How could we figure this out?*
   - *What was your thinking behind this answer?*
   - *How did you get to this solution?*

7. Tier 1: **Basic Questions** for *Identification & Labeling*
   - Straightforward *what* questions to encourage the child to name objects or characters in the story, for example: *What is the character doing?*
   - Expand opportunities to practice vocabulary.

8. Tier 2: **Open-Ended** *Descriptive Questions*
   - Encourage students to describe actions or events or explain simple cause-and-effect relationships, such as: *"Why is the character not satisfied with the buttons?"*
   - Require more than one-word answers, prompting the child to expand on their responses.

9. Tier 3: **Higher-order** *Abstract Thinking Questions*
   - Stimulate critical thinking and deeper comprehension by encouraging children to make *predictions*, infer *outcomes*, or *relate* the story to their own experiences, for example, *What do you think will happen next?*

10. **Use narratives to teach math vocabulary.**
    - Pre-teach vocabulary through play.
    - Use visuals in the book for support and/or additional images/objects.
    - Practice using new vocabulary through questions and discussions.
    - Connect vocabulary to real-world scenarios familiar to your students.
    - Reinforce with extension activities, such as role-playing.
    - Use vocabulary in different contexts.

11. **Ask analytical questions** to foster mathematical thinking. Pose open-ended questions during storytelling to enrich comprehension and promote a range of problem-solving strategies.
    - ***Predictive questions*** to encourage critical thinking and curiosity: *What will happen next? What types of math problems might the character face if the story continued?*

- **Descriptive questions** to incorporate math vocabulary and clarify understanding: *Can you describe the characters' actions, such as the shapes they create? Can you use math terms to explain or describe what happened in the story?*
- **Relational questions** to connect math to personal experiences: *Have you ever been in a situation similar to the characters'? Can you recall when you had to solve a problem like the characters? How do you use, for example, a math concept in your daily life?*
- **Exploratory questions** to promote creative thinking and examine various strategies or solutions: *What other ways could the characters tackle this problem? Can you conceive a method to resolve the issue without, for example, an item from the story? How would that function?*
- **Explanation questions** to articulate and clarify thought processes: *Why did the character or you choose to do this or use this math concept? What would you do differently?*
- **Imaginative and creative questions** to spark inspiration: *What if the character acted differently or if the circumstances changed? What would happen if the story's numbers, shapes, or items were altered? How would the character's solution differ? Can you come up with a new problem for the character to solve? What numbers, shapes, or other elements would you select?*
- **Reflection questions** to reinforce learning: *What math terms did we encounter today, and how did the characters use them? What was the most challenging part of the story, and how did the characters tackle it?* Students can share their insights with the group.
- **Empathy questions** to create emotional connections: *How do you think the character felt at this moment, for example, upon solving the problem? How might you help the character in this situation? What would you say or do? How does the character's mistake contribute to their learning and growth?*

12. **Build on children's ideas** by focusing on and affirming their unique thought processes and approaches rather than just the correct answers.

CHAPTER 7

Teachers as Math Storywriters

Stories take us inside a context where young mathematicians have opportunities to play, think, ask, and solve problems with meaning and sense-making.

—Hintz and Smith (2022)

EXPERIENCE

Let's Math-It!

We've all heard: *A picture is worth a thousand words!* Let's use a different lens and list *how many math ideas* this picture is worth!

Considered a classic of children's literature, *Little Red Riding Hood* (with its varied versions) involves a young girl wearing a red hood, a wolf, her mother, and her grandmother. Various versions take root from oral European folklore and the written versions of Charles Perrault (1697) and the Brothers Grimm (1812).

Activity:

1. Observe the picture and write as many math ideas as possible. Here's an example of a math idea: *There are infinite paths between two points.*
2. Rewrite the math idea into a question. *How can Little Red Riding Hood remember the fastest way to get to her grandmother's house?*

Reflection:

- The open-ended question leads to various responses. The image provides context for learning significant math concepts, such as measuring distance.
- Consider the potential responses children may have to open-ended questions. Logical connections with other mathematical concepts, such as counting, measurement, time, operations, and equations, may be raised.

This chapter introduces two ways to write math stories. Tailor your story to the grade level you teach.

- **Math-It:** Transform the classic tale of *Little Red Riding Hood* into a math-oriented story.
- **Write your math story with MathXplorers characters and settings.**

Objectives of writing a math story:

1. Address the *necessity* of transforming math sessions into active, meaningful, and productive learning experiences for children.
2. Foster *curiosity* and *creativity* by encouraging children to explore mathematical thinking while mastering specific state standards in math and other subjects.
3. Develop a *community* of math thinkers by helping children cooperatively understand math in various contexts. This will allow them to observe, reason, listen, articulate, and connect mathematical concepts to imaginative real-world applications.

MATH-IT: LITTLE RED RIDING HOOD

There are many different versions of this story that you can choose to build your own story. On his website https://sites.pitt.edu/~dash/type0333.html, Ashliman (2021) translated and edited different versions of the tale of *Little Red Riding Hood* as told in various countries. These include:

- *Little Red Riding Hood* (Charles Perrault)
- *Little Red Cap* (Jacob and Wilhelm Grimm)

- *Little Red Hood* (Germany/Poland)
- *Little Red Hat* (Italy/Austria)
- *The Grandmother* (France)
- *The True History of Little Golden-Hood* (Charles Marelles)
- *Red Ridinghood* (Ireland)
- *The Little Girl and Her Grandmother* (Ireland)
- *Red Riding Hood* (Ireland)
- *The Old Man and the Wolf* (Romania)

The story of *Little Red Riding Hood* is a classic fairy tale about a young girl named for the red cloak she wears. Her mother sends her to visit her sick grandmother, and along the way, she encounters a wolf who slyly asks her where she is going. Innocently, Little Red Riding Hood tells the wolf that she is headed to her grandmother's house (Ashliman, 2021).

The wolf hatches a plan and races ahead, arriving at the grandmother's house first. He tricks the grandmother, swallows her whole, and disguises himself in her clothes. When Little Red Riding Hood arrives, she is unaware of the wolf's deception but becomes suspicious as she notices her "grandmother" looks strange, commenting on her large ears, eyes, and teeth. Ultimately, the wolf reveals himself and tries to eat Little Red Riding Hood (Zipes, 1993).

In some versions of the story, a passing woodsman or hunter hears her cries for help and arrives just in time to rescue from the hungry wolf. He cuts the wolf open (or in other versions, the grandmother is rescued), and the wolf is punished for his actions, leaving Little Red Riding Hood wiser and more cautious for the future (Grimm, 1812; Perrault, 1697). The story is often seen as an instructive and cautionary tale about the dangers of talking to strangers (Tatar, 1999).

Rewrite the Tale into a Math Story

Make it relevant. Align your narrative and images to your students' ages and contexts. The following example is aimed at 3rd-graders, primarily children 8–9 years old.

Step 1. Describe Your Students, Your Readers. Typically, children at this age are becoming more aware of social connections. They choose and develop friendships with peers. Conflicts arising from different personality traits, preferences, cultural backgrounds, jealousy, expectations, and perspectives are more prevalent. On the other hand, they are growing in empathy and increasingly understand what it means to *feel* for the other.

Step 2. Determine Academic Benchmarks. This is an example of how the story can be aligned to 3rd-grade standards in math and reading.

3rd Grade	
Math https://www.thecorestandards.org/Math/	**Reading** https://www.thecorestandards.org/ELA-Literacy/
Through the School Year	
Explore multiplication and division, measurement, fractions, and geometry applications.	Transition to reading to learn (as opposed to earlier years when they are primarily learning to read) while continuing to expand their vocabulary and writing skills.
The Story of Little Red Riding Hood	
Measurement and Data	**Vocabulary Acquisition and Use**
Solve problems involving measurement and time.	Use a sentence as clue to the meaning of a word or phrase.
Algebraic Thinking	**Understand Word Meanings**
Multiply	**Words in Context**
Represent and solve problems with multiplication within 100.	Determine the meaning of math words and phrases used in a text.
Patterns	**Knowledge of Language**
Identify, code, and explain patterns.	Choose words and phrases to communicate ideas.
Data	**Integrate Language and Ideas**
Represent and interpret data.	Use information gained from illustrations and the words to articulate ideas.
Numeracy and Multiplication	**Communicate**
Base Ten Number and Operations	**Read and Build Sentences**
Use place value and properties of multiplication to perform multidigit operations.	Write and articulate simple, compound, and complex sentences.

Step 3. Retell the Narrative. Contemporizing tales involves updating or adapting traditional stories to reflect modern settings, values, or cultural norms while retaining the core elements of the original narrative. Contemporizing helps keep the original story's lessons and appeal while making it accessible and meaningful to newer generations. Here are some guidelines for contemporizing fairy tales:

Relevant messages should be developmentally appropriate, ensuring that the material is suitable for the student's age and stage of learning.

Meaningful stories relate the historical or fantastical settings of the original tale with contemporary meanings. Choosing representative aspects of the story retains the imaginative fairy-tale flavor but with intended significance for today's children.

Character adaptation involves modernizing the characters so children can relate to their traits, choices, abilities, and weaknesses.

Language and dialogue are updated to make the story more understandable for today's readers or listeners. Archaic terms or phrases are maintained for symbolic purposes or replaced with contemporary vocabulary.

Themes and morals are revised to address societal issues and values, aligning the story's message with modern concerns.

Technology integration modernizes with inventive gadgets that take on pivotal roles in the plot. Today's children grow up with gadgets. Instead of avoiding the topic, stories can inspire them to use technology for good.

Through contemporizing, fairy tales maintain their timeless essence with creative and symbolic elements and become more accessible and relevant to modern readers.

Contemporizing Little Red Riding Hood for 3rd-Graders	
Relevant Message	"You grandmother depends on you." Focus on the task.
Meaningful Stories	Setting is in the city, with the gadget as the modern big, bad wolf. Foster empathy and responsibility with children helping elderly family members using their knowledge and skills.
Character Adaptation	**Little Red Riding Hood** A tech-savvy 3rd-grader who lives in the city **Mother of Little Red Riding Hood** Single mom who needs to go to work every day **Grandmother** Has back pain from surgery and requires meal deliveries and walking for exercise **Big, Bad Wolf is the gadget** Causes distraction and child loses her way **Tom** A friend that loves to play video games
Themes and Morals and Technology Integration	Don't get distracted by video games. Use digital gadgets for good, like navigating your way and checking on grandmother's condition.

Step 4. Storyboard the Narrative by Determining the Key Scenes of the Story.

1. **Create the narrative structure.** Storyboarding helps you visualize the flow of the story, ensuring that key plot points are clearly defined and logically arranged. By outlining the key scenes, you can see how the story progresses from beginning to end, making it easier to identify and resolve any gaps or inconsistencies in the plot.
2. **Determine pacing and timing.** Ensure that critical moments receive the appropriate amount of story narrative and attention. At the same time, less significant parts contribute elements to the story, creating a balanced rhythm that keeps the audience engaged.
3. **Focus on the main themes and message.** Let the characters and mathematical ideas weave the plot as they unravel the main themes and messages. Intersect math ideas into the narrative to progressively elevate mathematical understanding.
4. **Ensure visual and emotional impact.** Determine how each scene looks and feels. Represent the mathematical ideas while taking note of how these create a visual and emotional impact on the audience.
5. **Sharpen language use with editing and revisions.** Visually developing the story with a storyboard helps spot areas needing revision or refinement. It streamlines the editing process by allowing you to rearrange or rework scenes. Keep editing until the ideas and the emotions are clearly communicated.

Little Red Riding Hood: A Modern City Tale

Scene 1   **Introduce the lead character.**
Once upon a time, a girl named Little Red Riding Hood lived in a bustling city. She loved playing games on her gadget. Little Red lived with her mother, a single mom who had to go to work all day every day.

Scene 2   **Establish the character's goal.**
One morning, Little Red's mom said, *I need you to take this meal to Grandma. She just had surgery, and her back hurts, so she can't cook. Also, take her to go for her daily walk.* Little Red nodded, grabbed her digital tablet, and clicked on the map.
Check out the map. Count how many street blocks from Little Red's to her Grandma's house.

Scene 3   **Forewarning signals.**
Grandma lived across the city, so Little Red had to navigate the busy streets. *Remember,* her mom warned, *stay focused on your task. It usually takes 30 minutes*

to walk to Grandma's house. Don't get distracted playing games. Use your tablet to get to Grandma's and check in with me when you arrive.

Estimate: How much time will Little Red need to get halfway to her Grandma's house? How many blocks will she have walked through the halfway point?

Scene 4   **Temptation.** As Little Red starts her journey, her friend Tom sends a message on her tablet, *"Hey, do you want to play that new game?"* She thinks for a moment but remembers her mother's warning. *"Maybe just one round,"* she thought.

How long does it take to play a game on the pad?
How long will it take Little Red get to her grandma's if she plays one game?

Scene 5   **Surrenders to weakness.** She opened the game, and before she knew it, an hour had passed! Like a sneaky wolf, the gadget had distracted her, and now she lost her way.

Little Red was lost and needed to walk three blocks to get back on track to her Grandma's. How many minutes would it take her to arrive?

Scene 6   **Distress on the horizon.** Meanwhile, Grandma was waiting for her lunch and daily walk, but Little Red Riding Hood was nowhere to be found.

Scene 7   **Epiphany.** Panicked, Little Red tried to figure out where she was. Her tablet's battery was low, and the streets looked unfamiliar. She realized playing the game kept her from focusing on her very important mission.

Scene 8   **Conquer weakness.** Little Red remembered her mother's advice: *Use digital gadgets for good.* She opened the digital map again and used it to navigate back on track.

(Image: Map to Grandma's house from Little Red's House and where she stood, three blocks away from the path.)

Soon after she saw the map, her gadget turned off.

Help Little Red get to her grandma's by texting her with the directions.

Scene 9   **Realization.** Once close to Grandma's, she quickly messaged her mom: *I got distracted, but I'm almost there!*

Scene 10   **Goal achieved.** Little Red finally arrives at Grandma's. She delivered the meal and set up her video chat. The family chatted together. Soon after Grandma ate her meal, she was ready to take a short walk with Little Red.

Scene 11   **Highlight lesson learned.** Grandma thanked Little Red. *You are good with gadgets, but remember, they are there to help us, not to lead us astray.*
How many tiles were on the seven street blocks that Little Red walked on?

Scene 12   **On her way home,** Little Red tells her friend Tom, *Gadgets can be helpful, but it's important not to let them distract you from what matters—like delivering food and caring for the people you love.*

How many tiles were added to the regular path from Little Red's to her Grandma's house?

How long will it take to walk halfway to her Grandma's?

Step 5. *Math-It!* In this step, you'll figure out how to scaffold mathematical thinking and problem-solving in your story! Here are more examples of math problems:

Scene 2

Math Idea: Represent and interpret data.

Option 1: Create an image guide. Tiles on sidewalks as "real-world" units of measurement.

How many steps will it take for Little Red to get to Grandma's house?

This is a sample illustration.

The Path to Grandma's House

Sample clue: 1 tile = 2 steps, 1 block = 10 tiles

Option 2: Children draw maps. Provide variables to practice representing and interpreting data. The learning goal is not (only) to get the correct answer. Children should formulate their equations from the data on the maps.

Sample variables:

- Little Red's house is seven blocks from Grandma's house.
- Visualize your units with square tiles on the streets.

Steps:

1. Distribute square-inch tiles for the children to use to calculate.
2. Children draw their maps of the city. This provides children with ownership of the problem.
3. Children work in pairs to create solutions.

Scene 5

Math idea: Solve problems involving measurement and estimate intervals of time. Use tiles as the unit of measurement. Children decide the value of X in the following:

$$1 \text{ Tile} = \mathbf{X} \text{ Steps } \textbf{(Distance)}$$
$$X \text{ Steps} = X \text{ Seconds } \textbf{(Time)}$$

Steps:

1. Start by asking a subjective question: *How much time did Little Red waste when she played games on her gadget?*
2. Encourage children to use the data from their experiences when playing games on their gadgets.
3. You will get different answers. Choose three answers. The answers will be used as variables for the next question.
4. Children will use any of the previous three answers to respond to the following question: *How long will it take Little Red to get to her Grandma's house when you include the time she wasted playing games on her gadget?*
5. Children work in pairs using the previously learned units of measurement and intersect these with the new math ideas and processes in the story. Learners can represent their answers with any one or more of the following: equations, illustrations, or graphs.
6. The results will determine how students use their previous knowledge to solve new math problems. Observe pairs at work to gauge how much additional scaffolding they need.
7. Students share and discuss their solutions with the class.

Scene 10

Math ideas: Identify and explain patterns in arithmetic. Use place value and properties of multiplication to perform multi-digit calculations.

Steps:

1. Instruct children to work in pairs to answer the question: *How much time would it have taken Little Red Riding Hood had she not played games along the way to her Grandma's house?*
2. Students must represent the solution in any one or more of the following: equations, illustrations, or graphs.
3. Each team presents to the class.
4. Discuss solutions and connect these to math ideas.

WRITE YOUR MATH STORY WITH MATHXPLORERS' CHARACTERS AND SETTINGS

To ignite your story-writing process, you will use the MathXplorers characters and the setting of the *Town of Whatever*. These are the steps to guide your writing process.

1. In your math story, *engage readers as active creators of their knowledge.* Children grow their math abilities when helping characters solve simulated real-world problems by exploring and discovering math concepts.

   Can you help the family determine which sides have the same and different lengths? Measure the sides of the triangles using strips of paper.

2. *Open-ended and context-driven math problems* offer students a more natural, connected, and engaging way to connect with mathematical concepts, allow for multiple approaches, and diminish math anxiety.

"Oh gosh, I must have made a mistake," says Maya. "Clothes need to have the same number of buttons and buttonholes."

How can Maya and Ramon solve this problem?

3. *Character dilemmas* cultivate readers' empathy and provide purpose for engaging in mathematical thinking.

4. *Scaffolding* prepares children to solve simple and complex problems. This pedagogical mechanism supports children's understanding of math ideas, problem-solving, and skills practice.

"The number of buttons and buttonholes must be *equal*," says Bikoy.
"My shirt has 2 buttons and 2 buttonholes."
He draws two buttons and two buttonholes. In between, he draws two lines: =.

5. *Mixing natural language* or conversational text helps with understanding mathematical vocabulary.

"I see," Manuel describes the tiles, "they are squares because they have **4** sides of the same length." Amyel is curious: "Does the word **inch** have anything to do with our rulers?"

6. The *relational aspect of math ideas* refers to how mathematical concepts are connected and relate to each other. When students understand these relationships, they can apply their knowledge more flexibly and meaningfully across different areas of math.
7. *Multicultural characters* create intercultural learning environments with multiple perspectives.
8. *Math is fun!* Compare the way children learn and behave between straightforward math lessons and math stories. The natural connections with stories make math teaching and learning more enjoyable and meaningful.

START WRITING!

Relating Math Ideas

Multiplication is a fundamental math operation that relates to many other mathematical concepts. Its connection to different areas of math helps students understand that math ideas are interrelated. Multiplication is often described as repeated addition. For example, instead of adding the number of apples in four baskets with three apples each, multiplication simplifies this as $3 \times 4 = 12$. Equations are expressions of equality and describe how numbers and functions operate. When we multiply, we use equations.

Understanding multiplication's relationship with addition, division, geometry, fractions, exponents, and more helps students build a solid mathematical foundation that prepares them for more advanced concepts. In math stories, multiplication applies across different math fields; students can grasp the versatility and importance of this operation in both academic and real-world contexts. When exploring multiplication, include related math ideas, such as addition, division, equations, and units of measurement and quantity.

What's the Math Story?

In what real-world situations do we apply math ideas, such as multiplication? Multiplication is used in many real-world scenarios, from everyday shopping and cooking to more complex situations like construction, travel, and finance situations. It helps simplify calculations, manage resources efficiently, and solve problems.

Here are some examples:

1. Shopping and Budgeting

When calculating the total cost of multiple items, multiplication helps determine how much you'll spend. For instance, if an item costs $10 and you buy 5, you can multiply 10×5 to determine the total cost, which is $50. If a pair of shoes costs $45, and you want to buy 3 pairs, you multiply $45 \times 3 = \$135$, and you get the total cost without having to add $45 + \$45 + \$45$.

2. Cooking and Baking

Recipes often require ingredients to be scaled up or down depending on the number of servings. Multiplication helps adjust the quantity of ingredients to meet the needs of a larger or smaller group. When a recipe calls for 2 cups of flour to serve 4 people, but you want to serve 8 people, multiply 2×2 (doubling the recipe) to get 4 cups of flour.

3. Fitness and Exercise

Multiplication helps track exercise routines. If you do a set of exercises multiple times, you can use multiplication to calculate your total number of repetitions or sets. For example, if you perform 15 push-ups per set and do 4 sets, multiply 15 by 4 to find that you've done 60 push-ups in total.

Choose Your Characters

Meet the MathXplorers!

Get to know the characters at MathXplorers.org.

These characters were created as creative simulations of children we encountered in our teaching practices. In our study, students explained how connections to one or more characters made them feel like they had a friend they could emulate and inspired them to explore math ideas.

Create an Imaginary Setting

Imagine these characters in your math story. What setting and situation are you going to put them in?

Storyboard: A Narrative with Text and Images

1	2	3
Character Introduction	**Opening Scene**	**Build Anticipation**
Briefly describe the main character with attributes that relate to the story. Introductory lines set the tone of the narrative.	Describe the setting with main character/s.	Introduce Problem 1. Review of math ideas. 2. Character's dilemma
4	**5**	**6**
Provide clues	**Tasks prepare for the bigger problem**	**Bigger problem emerges**
Guide children with math ideas and procedures to help solve Problem 1 with related math ideas.	Characters cooperate to solve Problem 1 integrating related math ideas.	A bigger problem arises setting the stage for introducing new math ideas.
7	**8**	**9**
Provide clues.	**Apply related math ideas in simulated real-world context.**	**Children explore ways to solve the problem.**
Guide children with math ideas and procedures to help solve Problem 1 with related math ideas.	Characters cooperate to solve Problem 2 with nonformal approaches	Expound on the solutions.
10	**11**	**12**
Explain upon how math is a solution to real-world problems.	**Highlight children as mathematical thinkers and team players.**	**Feel and think about overcoming challenges with math strategies.**
Describe how the math solutions help with the characters' challenges.	What happens when problems are solved by the MathXplorers (all the characters in the story)?	Thoughts and feelings of the characters after they solved the problems.

Each page or panel in the storyboard has to show a progression in action and emotion, helping young readers follow the story visually while keeping the text simple and engaging. Include open-ended questions that spark curiosity and encourage students to explore *what if* scenarios. For example, *What if we had one more guest at the dinner table—how would we share the pie?*

MATH STORIES TRANSFORM MATH LEARNING!

Teachers and parents can craft their own math stories expanding on children's interests, creatively tailoring lessons to specific needs or themes. By embedding math in a story, math becomes a part of an adventure or mystery. This invites curiosity about how the characters will solve the problem or what will happen next, making math exploration natural and exciting.

When children see math applied in stories that mirror real-life situations, it deepens their understanding and makes them curious about how math works in their lives, such as in cooking, shopping, or building.

Children working together to solve story problems fosters teamwork and communication, reinforcing that math is a shared, cooperative activity. Stories facilitate every child's participation regardless of their math abilities and can contribute ideas or solutions, helping build confidence and a sense of belonging. Children feel for the characters and naturally connect to their journeys.

Stories activate the imagination. Visualizing a character solving a problem or imagining how to divide up a feast brings math to life, making it fun and tangible. Stories make information stick. When math is woven into a narrative, children are more likely to remember the concepts because they are tied to emotions, characters, and events they care about.

CHAPTER 8

Assessment

Observing Children Learning

Gather Evidence:

What do you observe in the picture?

    Assessments are designed to support student learning and inform instructional design. The National Council of Teachers of Mathematics (NCTM) defines assessment as *gathering evidence* about a *student's knowledge* of, *ability to use*, and *disposition* toward mathematics and *making inferences from the evidence* for various purposes (NCTM, 1995). The following image illustrates four phases of developing assessments and reviewing findings.

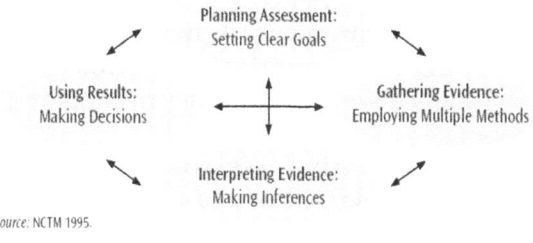

Planning Assessment:
Setting Clear Goals

Using Results:
Making Decisions

Gathering Evidence:
Employing Multiple Methods

Interpreting Evidence:
Making Inferences

Source: NCTM 1995.

1. How will you assess students' disposition toward math learning?
2. What inferences can you make from observing children as they learn through math stories?
3. How will you use the information you have to determine the gaps in the math curriculum?

Reflection:

In his 2014 article "Looking for Leverage: Issues of Classroom Research on Algebra for All," Alan Schoenfeld calls on educational researchers to explore classroom dynamics in multicultural environments to help bridge student achievement gaps. He highlights the increasing demand for quantitative literacy, as individuals today need to use quantitative tools to analyze real-world situations, make logical arguments, interpret data, make informed decisions on social and personal matters, and communicate effectively.

As society demands higher levels of mathematical competence, aligning assessment practices to enhance students' mathematical reasoning and understanding becomes essential. Assessments should prioritize fostering mathematical reasoning, critical thinking, and problem-solving skills.

How, then, can standardized assessments provide straightforward and quantifiable criteria for determining students' math levels?

This chapter examines how assessment in the context of math stories can foster the development of children's mathematical thinking skills. Key areas of focus include:

- **Comparing quantitative and qualitative assessments:** Analyzing the strengths and limitations of both assessment types in measuring mathematical understanding.
- **Incorporating the intuitive, integrative, and intercultural aspects of math stories into assessment design:** Exploring how these elements can be embodied in assessments to enrich students' mathematical experiences.
- **Aligning assessment with math stories as a strategy for developing mathematical thinking:** Investigating how assessments can be aligned with math stories to support growth in mathematical reasoning.
- **Utilizing qualitative assessments through lesson activities based on the math story of Little Red Riding Hood:** Intersecting a familiar narrative with unstructured problems and skills using RME theory as context for qualitative assessment.

- **Using qualitative assessments to reflect children's thought processes:** Examining how qualitative assessments can help children gain insight into their mathematical thinking.

COMPARING QUANTITATIVE AND QUALITATIVE ASSESSMENTS

Quantitative and standardized math assessments often adhere to rigid multiple-choice or single-answer formats that don't permit creative reasoning or alternative solutions. Many students find it challenging to recognize how math applies to real-world situations, causing assessments to feel detached from their interests and daily lives. The pressure of racing against the clock reinforces that math is about quick calculations rather than thoughtful reasoning. This disconnect strengthens the misconception that math is an abstract and challenging subject instead of a practical tool for problem-solving. Consequently, this leads to math avoidance, as students believe they are "not good at math" if they cannot recall information instantly.

Quantitative and qualitative assessment strategies offer distinct approaches to evaluating children's knowledge and skills. Here's a comparison of both in terms of fostering understanding, identifying abilities, and shaping mathematical thinking abilities:

Why Qualitative Assessments Are Seen as Less Scalable

Qualitative math assessments are often considered impractical for large-scale implementation due to their time-consuming and individualized nature. However, with strategic planning and the right tools, key elements of qualitative evaluation can be expanded efficiently. Educators can improve scalability by utilizing rubrics, group assessments, digital platforms, and hybrid models, making qualitative assessments more feasible in larger classrooms without sacrificing depth or insight.

Aspect	Quantitative	Qualitative
Focus	Accuracy, skills mastery, speed	Understanding, reasoning, and conceptual depth
Format	Standardized tests, multiple-choice, true/false	Open-ended questions, reflections, models, observations
Purpose	Measure skill level and correct answers	Analyze thought processes, reasoning, and applications
Data Type	Numeric scores or percentages	Descriptive insights, anecdotal notes, verbal/written feedback

(continued)

Aspect	Quantitative	Qualitative
Strengths	Efficient, test items have measurability criteria, scalable, useful for tracking progress	Deep insight into the learner's understanding and thinking
Limitations	May not reveal conceptual understanding and reasoning other than showing solutions	Time-intensive, subjective, not easily scalable

Challenges of Qualitative Assessments

1. **Time-Intensive**—Observing, discussing, and evaluating students individually is demanding, especially in large classrooms.
2. **Subjectivity**—Assessing reasoning and thought processes relies on interpretation, making standardization difficult.
3. **Labor-Intensive Grading**—Open-ended responses require more effort to evaluate than simple right-or-wrong answers, slowing the assessment process.
4. **Complex Data Analysis**—Unlike numerical scores, qualitative insights are more challenging to organize, compare, and scale effectively.

Scaling Qualitative Assessments

Strategic strategies can address scalability challenges:

1. **Rubrics for Consistency**—Standardized rubrics streamline evaluation, reducing subjectivity and enabling multiple teachers to assess students efficiently.
2. **Small Group Discussions**—Instead of one-on-one assessments, students explain their reasoning in groups, allowing teachers to observe and assess multiple learners simultaneously.
3. **Technology Integration**—Digital portfolios, voice recordings, and video explanations let students demonstrate their thinking asynchronously, easing the burden on teachers.
4. **Targeted Sampling**—Assessing a rotating sample of students or focusing on key moments throughout the year ensures meaningful qualitative insights without overwhelming educators.

INTUITIVE, INTEGRATIVE, AND INTERCULTURAL MATH STORY ASSESSMENTS

The assessment guidelines for math stories foster children's mathematical sense making and reasoning through intuitive, integrative, and intercultural approaches. By aligning the stories' contexts with the National Council of Teachers of Mathematics (NCTM) Principles and Standards, these guidelines aim to deepen students' understanding of mathematical concepts and nurture the potential of children from diverse and multicultural backgrounds.

Assessment should align with the learning materials. For example, to promote conceptual understanding, students can engage in critical and relational thinking methods instead of simply memorizing various shapes. The image below illustrates shape concepts through characters exploring a circle from the perspective of a triangle. Through discovery and exploration, children identify polygons as shapes with straight sides, contrasting them with circles, which lack straight sides.

The material enhances conceptual understanding and fosters students' natural abilities and interests in working with shapes. Students' skills extend beyond merely identifying shapes for assessment. They can construct shapes using various forms, a significant mathematical concept applicable to other fields such as science, engineering, technology, the arts, and design. Learning about shapes relationally is relevant and profound, paving the way for real-world and abstract applications of mathematical concepts.

"I'm trying to build a circle with triangles, but it's not working," says Kenneth.

Jessica is confused. "I can't find any sides or corners."

"That's because it doesn't have any, which means the circle is not a polygon," says Manuel.

How to Design More Intuitive Math Assessments

Math stories provide natural and accessible ways to learn math. Through relatable scenarios, the text and images embed mathematical ideas that reflect children's inherent understanding and lived experiences, so the learners engage with mathematical ideas emotionally and intellectually.

Making math assessments more intuitive should align with how students naturally think, explore, and apply mathematical concepts, rather than focusing solely on procedural accuracy. Educators can create assessments that foster understanding, engagement, and real-world relevance. Here are some strategies:

1. Frame problems in familiar and relatable story scenarios to make them more relatable.
2. Balance procedural and creative thinking by including open-ended questions that encourage students to explore patterns, make connections, and justify their reasoning.
3. Incorporate visual and interactive elements. Use graphs, charts, models, and manipulatives to help students visualize problems. Encourage students to show their reasoning through drawings, explanations, or multiple strategies. Digital assessments can enhance understanding by including drag-and-drop options, simulations, and interactive tools.

Here is a sample assessment utilizing a single problem that incorporates multiple math ideas.

Problem: The Mystery Tile Floor

Emma is designing a new tile floor for her playroom. She wants to use two colors of square tiles to make a pattern.

- Create a pattern
  - » Select 2 colors for Emma's tiles.
  - » Create a pattern for the floor that she can use.
- Extend the pattern
  - » Repeat the pattern every 4 tiles. What will the 10th tile be?
  - » Explain how you know this to be.
- Make a connection
  - » Emma decides to add another color to her pattern.
  - » How will this affect the pattern?
  - » Draw and then explain the pattern with letters A, B, and C, with each letter symbolizing a color.

This problem incorporates:

- **Procedural Thinking**—Pattern recognition, sequencing, and number reasoning.
- **Creative Thinking**—Allows students to choose colors, create designs, and explore variations.
- **Open-Ended Exploration**—There is no single correct *answer*; students explain their reasoning and patterns.
- **Relational Thinking**—Expands thinking by asking how adding another element affects the pattern.

By integrating meaningful contexts, various solution methods, interactive components, and a conceptual focus, educators can design assessments that empower students to think mathematically instead of merely performing calculations.

Integrative Dimensions of Math Stories

Math stories blend elements, including characters, narratives, and images, to captivate children's interest. Concrete scenarios scaffold the path to understanding abstract ideas, allowing children to transfer and apply math concepts to imaginative real-world contexts. Moreover, mathematical vocabulary is seamlessly interspersed in the characters' dialogues, illuminating quantitative, logical, and spatial ideas with familiar language.

Intercultural Dimensions of Math Stories

Recognizing students' diverse backgrounds, intercultural math stories draw from multicultural experiences. Stories with characters representing a mix of cultures and open-ended problems offer opportunities for multiple perspectives, providing examples for children to build a shared understanding of mathematical concepts across cultures.

Aligning Assessment with Math Stories

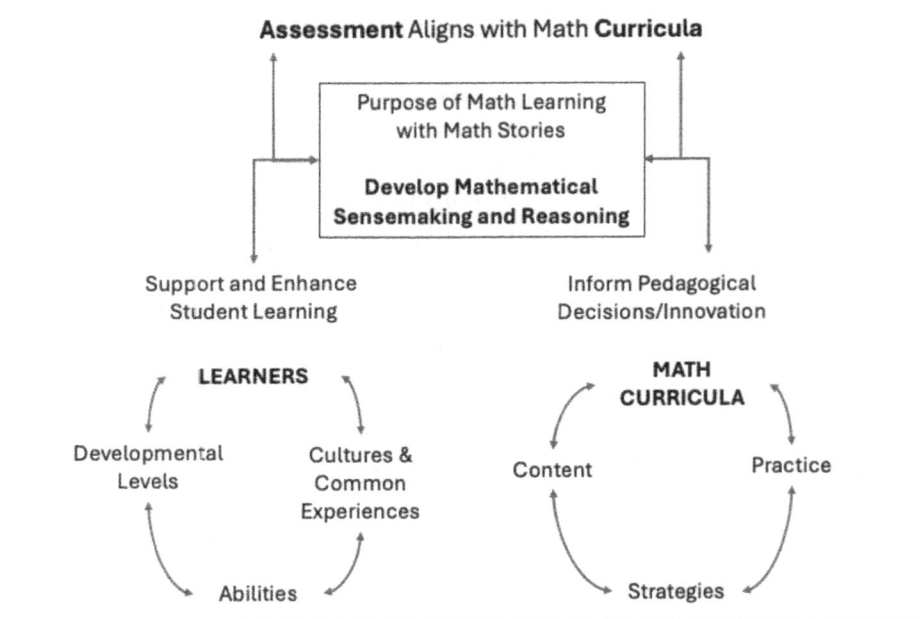

MATH STORIES AND MATH CURRICULA

Math stories are structured as a teaching strategy to foster mathematical sensemaking and reasoning. The math concepts embedded within these stories are carefully scaffolded to guide students from simple to more complex understandings, much like a lesson plan.

Solutions to the problems in math stories draw on students' background knowledge and experiences, integrating multiple mathematical concepts and procedures to enhance their understanding of mathematical reasoning. Through these approaches, children engage with:

1. **Content**: Exploring relational aspects of math concepts within a story context.
2. **Strategies**: Solving context-driven dilemmas that encourage problem-solving.
3. **Practice**: Interacting with and applying math concepts in meaningful ways.

MATHEMATICAL SENSEMAKING

Mathematical sensemaking and reasoning enable students to understand, interpret, and apply mathematical concepts meaningfully.

In math stories, sensemaking involves understanding how mathematical ideas work to understand, solve problems, and predict issues in context. Children instinctively weave prior knowledge when observing, figuring out, and analyzing concepts, relationships, and problems in real-world contexts and familiar situations.

When engaged in mathematical sensemaking, a student might recognize multiplication as counting equal groups rather than memorizing the times tables. This understanding enables them to approach multiplication problems flexibly and apply the concept in different contexts.

There are 2 scoops of ice cream in each cone.
There are 4 cones.
2 scoops × **4** cones = **8** scoops in **4** cones of ice cream

Sensemaking also involves identifying patterns, connecting concepts, and visualizing problems using graphs, diagrams, or physical models. It's about creating a mental model of math that makes it intuitive and conducive to authentic comprehension.

As Blum and Niss (1991) describe, mathematical modeling uses different strategies to solve problems without relying on a single procedure. This process integrates the learner's background knowledge and mathematical principles relevant to the task. According to Lehrer and Schäuble (2003), models include representations, operations, and relationships that help make sense of real-life scenarios.

A Math Story Example

Iliana and Ruby are using their favorite counting strategy.
"Let's group the tiles in each room into sets of 10. Then count how many there are," says
Iliana. "I love counting by 10s!" sings Ruby.

Ruby, the ice-cream maker, uses her understanding of grouping and skip counting by tens and ones to calculate the total number of tiles for a floor plan. Her strategy is a segue to multiplication as repeated addition—combining equal groups to calculate the total or Sum. Ruby realizes she can compute for the sum when she combines multiplication and addition and does this with the support of skip counting by tens.

Sensemaking strengthens students' logical thinking about math concepts, helping them solve problems independently and apply mathematics meaningfully. As Verschaffel et al. (2002) note, sensemaking through mathematical modeling mathematically represents an understanding of real-world situations.

REALISTIC MATHEMATICS EDUCATION AND ASSESSMENT IN MATH STORIES

One of the inspirations for the math stories dismcussed in this book is the theory of realistic mathematical education (RME). Freudenthal (1973), the creator, is critical of traditional top-down math education. He explains that one learns mathematics only through *mathematizing*. In RME, sensemaking or mathematical modeling, also called *mathematizing*, has two main parts:

vertical and horizontal components. Treffers (1978) and Freudenthal (1991) distinguish between *horizontal mathematization*, describing the process as "leads from the world of life to the world of symbols," and *vertical mathematization* as engaging math with the system of mathematics.

Heuvel-Panhuizen (2000) explains that learners generate meaningful mathematics to solve real-life problems when informal and formal knowledge intersect. In this regard, we will utilize the steps outlined by Üzel (2007) in horizontal mathematization to create a sample rubric for qualitative assessment.

Process/Steps	Description	Math Story Application
Apply	Address and structure problems connected to real-world scenarios with known and newly learned mathematics tools. *Mathematical Application*: Distance measurement, route optimization, and time estimation.	Little Red Riding Hood uses a city map and a distance-measuring app on her phone to determine the shortest path to her Grandma's house. She also notes the time it takes to cross each city block, helping her estimate how long the entire journey will take.
Contextualize	Structure and communicate mathematical ideas within a particular context. *Mathematical Application*: Time intervals, sequencing, and predicting patterns.	To cross busy intersections safely, Little Red Riding Hood calculates the wait times for traffic lights at crosswalks. She expresses the duration of each light cycle (30 seconds for the green light and 60 seconds for the red light) in mathematical terms, helping her predict when to cross.
Represent and organize the problem	Mathematically organize the problem using different approaches and viewpoints. *Mathematical Application*: Map representation, grid visualization, and spatial reasoning.	To avoid getting lost again, Little Red Riding Hood sketches a quick map of her route, marking important locations like intersections, buildings, and parks. She represents each block as a square and shows the crosswalks as lines connecting the blocks, which allows her to visualize the path and estimate the total distance.
Explore and express connections	Transform the scenario into mathematical expressions. *Mathematical Application*: Review her trip and calculate how much time she would have saved had she not played games on her gadget.	On her way home, Little Red Riding Hood realizes she could have had more time with her Grandma had she not gotten distracted with playing games.

HORIZONTAL MATHEMATIZATION + SENSEMAKING WITH LITTLE RED RIDING HOOD

Little Red is walking to Grandma's house and wants to know how far she has to walk. She counts the square tiles on the path to measure the distance. She also wants to know how long her journey will take if she walks at a steady pace.

Part A: Horizontal Mathematization

Children connect math to a familiar story, using physical counting, movement, and story scenarios to understand distance and time.

1. Assessing understanding of distance with tiles

Story: Little Red counts 12 tiles from her house to a big tree. Then she walks 8 more tiles to her Grandma's house. How many tiles long is her entire path?
Task: Draw the path. Count and write the number of tiles.

2. Explore the relationship between time and tiles

Story #1: If Little Red takes 1 second to walk on each tile, how many seconds will it take her to reach her Grandma's house? If she starts walking at 3:00 PM, what time will she arrive?
Task: Count and write the time in seconds, minutes, and hours.
Story #2: Little Red is distracted by her friend and she loses her way. Her new path has 5 extra tiles. How far will she need to walk to her Grandma's house? How much longer will her trip take?
Task: Explain your thinking by showing how you counted the tiles and created a solution.

Part B: Vertical Mathematization

Children are encouraged and guided to structure their thinking through equations and general patterns, transitioning from informal strategies to formal representations.

- Use equations to show the total distance. For example, $12 + 8 = 20$ tiles.
- Use equations to show the total travel time. For example, 20 tiles $\times$ 1 second for each tile $= 20$ seconds.
- When Little Red is distracted and has to take a path with 5 additional tiles: $20 + 5 = 25$ tiles.
- and 25×1 second $= 25$ seconds.

Part C: The Rubric for Qualitative Assessment

A rubric provides a structured and transparent framework for evaluating students' responses to both horizontal and vertical mathematization questions in a qualitative assessment. Defining clear criteria helps educators systematically assess students' understanding, reasoning, and problem-solving processes.

Criteria	4 Advanced	3 Proficient	2 Basic	1 Emerging
Understands Time Intervals	Accurately calculates time intervals in complex, multistep problems and explains reasoning clearly.	Calculates time intervals in straightforward situations and provides basic explanations.	Calculates time intervals with some guidance; explanations are limited or partially accurate.	Struggles to calculate time intervals even with guidance; explanations are incomplete or inaccurate.
Sequencing of Steps	Develops a logical sequence for complex, real-life problems with minimal assistance.	Creates a logical sequence of steps for straightforward problems; may need minor support.	Develops a sequence of steps with guidance; order may have some loopholes.	Struggles to organize steps into a logical sequence even with guidance.
Predicting Patterns	Identifies and predicts complex patterns accurately and can apply these patterns to new contexts or real-life scenarios.	Recognizes and predicts basic patterns in familiar contexts; occasionally applies patterns to new problems.	Recognizes simple patterns with guidance but struggles to predict outcomes accurately.	Has difficulty identifying or predicting patterns, even with guidance.
Use of Known Math Tools	Effectively applies known math tools to structure and solve real-world problems; adapts tools to new scenarios.	Applies known math tools accurately to solve familiar problems; may need support to apply tools to new contexts.	Uses math tools with guidance; applies tools inconsistently or with limited understanding in real-world contexts.	Limited use or understanding of math tools; struggles to apply tools to real-world scenarios even with guidance.

(continued)

Criteria	4 Advanced	3 Proficient	2 Basic	1 Emerging
Use of Newly Learned Math Tools	Confidently incorporates new math tools into problem-solving; adapts them to structure problems in various contexts.	Uses new math tools correctly with guidance in familiar contexts; attempts to use them in new scenarios.	Uses new tools with significant guidance; applies them inconsistently in solving problems.	Struggles to incorporate new math tools, even in familiar contexts, and requires significant guidance.
Problem Structuring and Solving	Independently structures complex, real-world problems; integrates various tools and approaches seamlessly.	Structures straightforward real-world problems effectively; integrates familiar tools with minor guidance.	Structures problems with guidance; attempts to integrate tools but may lack coherence in approach.	Struggles to structure problems, even with guidance; limited integration of tools and lack of coherent approach.

MATHEMATICAL REASONING

Mathematical reasoning integrates logic and creative thinking to explore mathematical ideas, solve problems, and justify solutions. It employs a logical process to reach conclusions using variables, parameters, definitions, properties, and previously proven methods and concepts.

While sensemaking involves interpreting the situation, reasoning is solving it and understanding how different elements fit together. Freudenthal (1991) and Gravemeijer and Stephan (2002) describe modeling as more than simply translating real-life problems into mathematical terms; it's about uncovering the relationships within situations by organizing their elements. Learners begin with real-world contexts and intuitively develop frameworks to interpret the connections between variables. Cobb (2002) clarifies that "modeling" encompasses both the mathematical representations of the scenario and components of students' conceptual understanding.

Mathematical reasoning includes:

- **Logical thinking:** Using deductive or inductive reasoning to conclude.
- **Justifying answers:** Providing a rationale or proof for why a solution works.

- **Making inferences:** Drawing conclusions based on patterns, given information, or assumptions.
- **Building arguments:** Constructing coherent explanations that validate the reasoning process.

Examples:
Multiplication is a form of repeated addition.
$4 + 4 + 4 + 4 + 4 = 20$
5 groups of 4 add up to 20.
So, 5 4 is the same as adding 4 five times.
The Commutative Property applies to
Multiplication:
5 groups of 4 will have the exact total as 4 groups of 5.
$5 \times 4 = 4 \times 5$

Addition:
5 added to 4 will have the exact total as 4 added to 5.
$5 + 4 = 4 + 5$

A Math Story Example

"I see," says Bikoy, "These numbers tell us which columns have
10 tiles. This way, we can quickly count the area by 10s."

In the preceding example, Bikoy (the story character) explains his solution and method for calculating the total number of tiles used in the floor plan based on his observations of the tiles and previous knowledge of skip counting. Noticing the pattern of ten tiles in each column and relating this to counting by tens reflects a child-driven perspective solving for area. Observing the same number patterns and skip counting indicates the child is ready to explore multiplication and learn about the formula for calculating area.

Mathematization + Reasoning With Little Red Riding Hood

These rubric components provide a structured way to assess various aspects of a learner's mathematical reasoning and problem-solving in real-life contexts, giving insight into practical and conceptual math skills.

- **Use of mathematical tools in solving real-life problems:** Assesses the learner's ability to apply practical tools like maps to navigate and estimate time and distance.

- **Visualization and formalization of the problem:** Looks at the learner's skill in creating a map or diagram to represent spatial relationships, helping in route planning.
- **Exploring and expressing relationships in real-life problems:** Assesses the ability to figure out how to manage time as this relates to distance.
- **Problem transformation and mathematical representation:** Measures the skill in translating real-life scenarios into mathematical models, like route optimization and equations as evidence of thinking.
- **Predicting patterns and making decisions based on reasoning:** Evaluates the student's ability to observe, predict, and apply patterns to make informed and responsible decisions.

Sample Rubric for Mathematical Reasoning

Criteria	4 Advanced	3 Proficient	2 Basic	1 Emerging
Use of Math Tools in Solving Real-Life Problems	Effectively uses math tools (maps, apps) to find the optimal path; estimates time accurately for a complex route.	Uses math tools appropriately to determine a reasonable path and make basic time estimates.	Attempts to use tools with some guidance; estimates time but with limited accuracy.	Struggles to use tools effectively or to estimate time accurately even with assistance.
Visualizing and Formalizing the Problem	Creates a detailed, accurate map with key locations and connections; demonstrates clear spatial reasoning in path planning.	Draws a basic map with important locations and pathways; applies spatial reasoning in choosing a path.	Sketches a simple map but may lack important details; spatial reasoning in path selection is limited and requires help.	Struggles with visualizing or creating a map, even with guidance; lacks spatial reasoning in choosing a path.
Problem Transformation and Mathematical Representation	Transforms real-life scenarios into math models.	Transforms scenarios into simple mathematical models; interprets results with general understanding.	Partially translates scenarios into mathematical models with guidance; interpretation of results is limited.	Struggles with transforming scenarios into mathematical models and lacks understanding in interpreting results.

Sample Rubric for Mathematical Reasoning (*continued*)

Criteria	4 Advanced	3 Proficient	2 Basic	1 Emerging
Predicting Patterns and Making Decisions Based on Reasoning	Consistently predicts light cycles and adjusts timing accordingly; makes logical decisions based on observed patterns.	Recognizes and uses basic patterns (e.g., light cycles) to inform safe crossing and other decisions.	Identifies some patterns with guidance but has difficulty using them effectively in decision-making.	Struggles to identify or apply patterns for safe and logical decisions, even with guidance.

BEYOND GRADES: CULTIVATING MATHEMATICAL THINKERS THROUGH MEANINGFUL ASSESSMENT

Quizzes, Tests, and Assessments and Math Anxiety

Math anxiety is a **fear or apprehension** about engaging with mathematics, often stemming from **negative experiences with quizzes, tests, and standardized assessments**. While intended to measure learning, these evaluation methods can unintentionally create stress and discourage students from developing confidence in math. Quizzes and tests often carry significant **grades and consequences**, making students feel that their **ability is being judged** rather than their learning assessed. Many traditional assessments focus on **memorizing formulas, rules, and procedures**, rather than encouraging **conceptual understanding and problem-solving**. When students rely on memorization without grasping underlying concepts, they may **freeze under pressure** if they forget a step or formula. Receiving a low grade on a test may **create shame** or lead students to believe they lack mathematical ability.

Embracing Diverse Perspectives in Math Learning

Effective math assessments shape children's interest in the subject. Traditional tests, focused on memorization, procedural mastery, and textbook-driven correctness, often leave lasting emotional imprints that stifle curiosity and build anxiety. Standardized assessments further narrow mathematical understanding by emphasizing rule-following over exploration, diminishing engagement with math as a creative and dynamic discipline.

Assessments should go beyond measuring proficiency in formulas and problem-solving; they should cultivate curiosity, encourage experimentation, and deepen conceptual engagement. By broadening their purpose, educators can create learning environments that value accuracy, creative and logical reasoning, and discovery.

Incorporating open-ended problems, exploratory tasks, and real-world applications fosters flexible thinking and innovation. This approach strengthens mathematical skills and highlights the relevance and beauty of math in everyday life. Shifting the focus from performance to curiosity and creativity-driven exploration can inspire a lifelong enthusiasm for math learning.

Math stories naturally engage children by combining creativity, logic, and empathy. They allow students to explore math in a way that resonates with their cultural backgrounds and personal experiences. Children feel motivated, empowered, and fulfilled in this dynamic, collaborative learning environment. Math becomes more than a subject; it's a journey of meaning-making supported by assessments that value students' unique insights. Through math stories, we foster communities of curious, creative, and diverse learners who see their own experiences and perspectives reflected in their education.

Epilogue

As a means to learn mathematics, stories facilitate and enrich understanding by explaining and illustrating mathematical concepts and processes through engaging narratives. The children in our study, who come from diverse backgrounds, expressed interest and joy in learning math through these stories. They asked if they could take the math storybooks home to share with their parents. By blending numbers, patterns, and open-ended problem-solving into relatable and imaginative contexts, math stories sparked their curiosity, inspired creativity, and made abstract ideas more accessible. When integrated into math lessons, we observed how picture-book narratives created interactive learning experiences that encouraged children to assist the characters and, in the process, reduce their anxiety about learning math. Students perceived mathematics as dynamic and meaningful, contrasting with their earlier sentiment of "math is difficult" at the onset of the study. By learning to model mathematically, the children reached a state of flow and developed the ability to transfer knowledge, enriching their conceptual understanding.

MEANINGFUL, FULFILLING, AND JOYFUL MATH LEARNING

Creating meaningful, fulfilling, and joyful math learning experiences is essential for engaging students and fostering a positive attitude toward the subject. When students discover personal relevance, a sense of achievement, and enjoyment in learning math, they are more likely to develop a lasting interest in logical, quantitative, and spatial reasoning.

Meaningful. Through math stories, children connected mathematical concepts to real-life situations and personal experiences through relatable and inspiring imaginative themes. By linking mathematical ideas to students' lives, experiences, and interests, we emphasized the "why" behind these concepts, and students recognized the value of math education. The teachers pointed out how stories inspired their students to solve problems actively when faced with abstract math concepts in context.

Fulfilling. Connected experiences helped the children feel accomplished as they tackled challenges, offered valuable solutions, and received peer recognition. Students' active participation showed us that when math learning is purposeful, it encourages learners to recognize the positive results of their efforts, fostering an appreciation for persistence in problem-solving. We learned how a fulfilling math experience inspired learners by providing opportunities for problem-solving, critical thinking, and creativity. They applied mathematical concepts and procedures to situations to assist the characters in the story. Math learning through stories sparked their curiosity, creativity, and analytical thinking while also yielding the satisfaction of mastering complex concepts. Through this process, children cultivate resilience, perseverance, and a sense of agency.

Joyful. Learning math can be just as playful and exciting as it is challenging. Math stories that include scaffolded learning activities, such as games, puzzles, and design challenges, turned learning into a creative adventure. Enjoyable math experiences lessened anxiety and made it easier for students to tackle difficult problems with a positive mindset. We noticed that students who enjoyed learning math were engaged, curious, and eager to experiment with problem-solving.

Math Stories Shift the Way Children Perceive Math

The way we teach influences how children perceive their ability to learn mathematics. An increasing number of studies in the learning sciences highlight the lasting impact of pedagogy on how and what children learn. For the most part, math and literature have been taught separately and continue to be so. Clearly, in the case of math stories, engaging and creative narratives enhance the explanation and application of mathematical concepts and operations.

Mathematical Thinking Opens New Pathways for Success

Mathematical thinking is not merely an academic skill but a critical tool for success and innovation in an era driven by technology, data, and problem-solving. The ability to analyze patterns, reason logically, and approach problems systematically is essential in a world that requires adaptability, creativity, and sound decision-making. Individuals who can think mathematically can deconstruct complex issues, identify underlying structures, and create innovative solutions. Mathematical reasoning enables people to interpret data, assess trends, and make informed decisions in today's world, where big data and analytics impact nearly every industry.

Intercultural math stories humanize and offer a learner-oriented approach to math education. Contrary to the misconception that math is rigid, static, and solely dependent on memorization and repetitive practice, math stories enable children to discover how mathematical thinking fosters creativity through modeling. By exploring various approaches, recognizing patterns, and constructing logical arguments, these contexts illustrate that math is indeed everywhere, embedded in everyday situations. More importantly, there are multiple ways to solve problems mathematically. The characters in math stories illustrate that mathematical thinking is vital to enriching people's cultures in the modern world. Creative narratives offer children positive and insightful experiences that improve their abilities to reason, analyze, and solve problems mathematically. Intercultural math stories empower today's learners to engage across cultures and succeed in a world increasingly driven by mathematical literacy, where they can innovate, seize opportunities, and realize their boundless potential.

References

1001 Inventions. (n.d.). *Silk Road cities.* https://www.1001inventions.com/silk-road
-cities/

an den Heuvel-Panhuizen, M. (2003). The didactical use of models in realistic mathematics education: An example from a longitudinal trajectory on percentage. *Educational Studies in Mathematics, 54*(1), 9–35.

Anderson, L. W., & Krathwohl, D. R. (Eds.). (2001). *A taxonomy for learning, teaching, and assessing: A revision of Bloom's taxonomy of educational objectives.* Longman.

Arnold, E. G., Burroughs, E. A., Carlson, M. A., Fulton, E. W., & Wickstrom, M. H. (2021). *Becoming a teacher of mathematical modeling, K–Grade 5.* National Council of Teachers of Mathematics.

Ashcraft, M. H. (2002). Math anxiety: Personal, educational, and cognitive consequences. *Current Directions in Psychological Science, 11,* 181–185.

Ashcraft, M. H., & Moore, A. M. (2009). Mathematics anxiety and the affective drop in performance. *Journal of Psychoeducational Assessment, 27*(3), 197–205.

Ashliman, D. L. (2021). *Little Red Riding Hood tales: From around the world.* University of Pittsburgh. https://sites.pitt.edu/~dash/type0333.html

Association pour la diffusion de l'information archéologique/Royal Belgian Institute of Natural Sciences, Brussels (n.d.). "Have You Heard of Ishango?" Natural Sciences. Author.

Avanti Systems. (n.d.) https://www.avantisystemsusa.com/architecture-differences
-across-cultures

Bal, P. M., & Veltkamp, M. (2013). How does fiction reading influence empathy? An experimental investigation on the role of emotional transportation. *PLOS One, 8*(1), e55341. https://doi.org/10.1371/journal.pone.0055341

Baykul, Y. (2005). İlköğretimde matematik öğretimi (1–5.sınıflar için) [Teaching mathematics in primary education (for grades 1–5)]. Pegem A.

Berggren, J. L. (1985). "The Influence of Arabic Mathematics on Medieval Europe." *Historia Mathematica, 12*(3), 229–244.

Bishop, R. S. (1990). *Mirrors, windows, and sliding glass doors. Perspectives: Choosing and Using Books for the Classroom, 6*(3), ix–xi.

Blazer, C. (2011). Strategies for reducing math anxiety [Information capsule]. Retrieved February 19, 2018, from https://eric.ed.gov/?id=ED536509.

Bloom, B. S., Engelhart, M. D., Furst, E. J., Hill, W. H., & Krathwohl, D. R. (eds.) (1956). Taxonomy of educational objectives: the classification of educational goals. Handbook I: cognitive domain. David McKay.

Blum, W., & Niss, M. (1991). Applied mathematical problem-solving, modeling, application, and links to other subjects, trends, and issues in mathematics instruction. *Educational Studies in Mathematics, 22*(1), 37–68.

Boaler, J. (2016). *Mathematical mindsets: Unleashing students' potential through creative math, inspiring messages, and innovative teaching.* Jossey-Bass.

Bongiorno, L. (n.d.). *10 things every parent should know about play.* National Association for the Education of Young Children. https://www.naeyc.org/our-work/families/10-things-every-parent-play

Bransford, J. D., & B. S. Stein. (1993). *The IDEAL Problem Solver* (2nd ed.). Freeman.

Calinger, R. (1995). *Classics of mathematics.* Prentice Hall.

Carter, P. L., & Welner, K. G. (Eds.). (2013). *Closing the opportunity gap: What America must do to give every child an even chance.* Oxford University Press.

Casey, B. (2004). Mathematics problem-solving adventures: A language-arts-based supplementary series for early childhood that focuses on spatial sense. In D. H. Clements & J. Sarama (Eds.), *Engaging young children in mathematics: Standards for early childhood mathematics education* (pp. 377–389). Lawrence Erlbaum Associates.

Chestnut, E. K., Lei. R. F., Leslie, S. J., & Cimpian, A. (2018). The Myth That Only Brilliant People Are Good at Math and Its Implications for Diversity. *Education Sciences, 8*(2), 65. https://doi.org/10.3390/educsci8020065

Choe, K. W., Jenifer, J. B., Rozek, C. S., Berman, M. G., & Beilock, S. L. (2019). Calculated avoidance: Math anxiety predicts math avoidance in effort-based decision-making. *Science Advances, 5*(11), eaay1062. https://doi.org/10.1126/sciadv.aay1062

Clements, D. H., Sarama, J., & MacDonald, B. L. (2019). Subitizing: The neglected quantifier. In N. Anderson & M. W. Alibali (Eds.), *Constructing number: Merging perspectives from psychology and mathematics education* (pp. 13–45). Springer. https://link.springer.com/chapter/10.1007/978-3-030-00491-0_2

Cobb, P. (2002). Modeling, symbolizing, and tool use in statistical data analysis. In K. Gravemeijer, R. Lehrer, B. Van Oers, & L. Verschaffel (Eds.), *Symbolizing, modeling and tool use in mathematics education* (Mathematics Education Library, vol 30, pp. 171–195). Springer. https://doi.org/10.1007/978-94-017-3194-2_11

Corry, L. (2025). *Islamic contributions.* Brittanica. https://www.britannica.com/science/algebra/Islamic-contributions

Crawford, P. A., Roberts, S. K., & Lacina, J. (2024). Picturebooks and young children: Potential, power, and practices. *Early Childhood Education Journal.* https://doi.org/10.1007/s10643-024-01701-0

Csikszentmihalyi, M. (1996). *Creativity: Flow and the psychology of discovery and invention.* Harper Perennial.

Darwin, C. (1859). *On the origin of species by means of natural selection, or preservation of favoured races in the struggle for life.* John Murray.

Davydov, V. V., & Markova, A. K. (1983). A concept of educational activity for schoolchildren. *Soviet Psychology, 21*(2), 50–76.

DearDorff, D. K. (2020). *Manual for developing intercultural competencies: Story circles.* Routledge.

Deci, E. L., & Ryan, R. M. (2000). The "what" and "why" of goal pursuits: Human needs and the self-determination of behavior. *Psychological Inquiry, 11*(4), 227–268. https://doi.org/10.1207/S15327965PLI1104_01

Delpit, L. D. (1988). The silenced dialogue: Power and pedagogy in educating other people's children. *Harvard Educational Review, 58*(3), 280–298.

Devlin, K. (2011). *The man of numbers: Fibonacci's arithmetic revolution.* Walker & Company.

Dewey, J. (1902). *The child and the curriculum.* Chicago: University of Chicago Press.

Dixit, A., & Ndlovu-Gatsheni, S. J. (2019). Decolonizing mathematics: A history of mathematics without a central authority. *African Historical Review, 51*(1), 34–53.

Everett, C. (2017). *Numbers and the making of us: Counting and the course of human cultures.* Harvard University Press.

Fabina, J., Hernandez, E. L., & McElrath, K. (2023, June). *School enrollment in the United States: 2021.* American Community Survey Reports, ACS-55.

Fantini, A. E. (2006). *Exploring and assessing intercultural competence.* Federation of the Experiment in International Living.

Frankopan, P. (2015). *The Silk Roads: A new history of the world.* Bloomsbury Publishing.

Freudenthal, H. (1968). Why to teach mathematics so as to be useful. *Educational Studies in Mathematics, 1*(1), 3–8.

Freudenthal, H. (1973). *Mathematics as an educational task.* Reidel Publishing.

Freudenthal, H. (1991). *Revisiting mathematics education: China lectures.* Kluwer Academic Publishers.

Furner, J. M., & Berman, B. T. (2003). Review of research: Math anxiety: Overcoming a major obstacle to the improvement of student math performance. *Childhood Education, 79*(3), 170–174. https://doi.org/10.1080/00094056.2003.10522220

Ganley, C. M., Schoen, R. C., LaVenia, M., & Tazaz, A. M. (2019). Construct validation of the Math Anxiety Scale for Teachers. *AERA Open, 5*(1), 1–16.

Gardner, J. (1984). *The art of fiction: Notes on craft for young writers.* Vintage Books.

Gravemeijer, K., & Stephan, M. (2002). Emergent models as an instructional design heuristic. In K. Gravemeijer, R. Lehrer, B. Oers, & L. Verschaffel (Eds.), *Symbolizing, modeling and tool use in mathematics education* (pp. 145–169). Dordrecht, The Netherlands: Kluwer Academic Publishers.

Gravemeijer, K.P.E. (1994). *Developing realistic mathematics education.* CD-B Press / Freudenthal Institute.

Grimm, J., & Grimm, W. (1812). *Grimm's fairy tales.*

Gutiérrez, R. (2018). Introduction: The need to rehumanize mathematics. In I. Goffney, R. Gutiérrez, & M. Boston (Eds.), *Rehumanizing mathematics for Black, Indigenous, and Latinx students: Annual Perspectives in Mathematics Education, Vol. 2018* (pp. 1–10). National Council of Teachers of Mathematics.

Hagan-Howe, C. (2024). All about subitizing. All Learners Network. https://www.alllearnersnetwork.com/blog/subitizing

Harper, D. (2024). Tally. *Online Etymology Dictionary.* https://www.etymonline.com/word/tally

Hartnett, D., & Koepfle, L. (2011, Fall). Exploring the Rhind papyrus. *Ohio Journal of School Mathematics, 64.*

Haven, K. (2007). *Story proof: The science behind the startling power of story.* Libraries Unlimited.

Hiebert, J., & Grouws, D. A. (2007). The effects of classroom mathematics teaching on students' learning. In F. K. Lester Jr. (Ed.), *Second handbook of research on mathematics teaching and learning* (pp. 371–404). Information Age Publishing.

Hintz, A., & Smith, A. (2022). *Mathematizing children's literature,* Kindle Edition. Stenhouse Publishers.

Hmelo-Silver, C. E. (2004). Problem-based learning: What and how do students learn? *Educational Psychology Review, 16*(3), 235–266. https://doi.org/10.1023/B:EDPR.0000034022.16470.f3

Hofstede, G. (2001). *Culture's consequences: Comparing values, behaviors, institutions, and organizations across nations.* Sage Publications.

Huylebrouck D., (1996). The bone that began the space odyssey. *The Mathematical Intelligencer, 18*(4), 56–60.

Huylebrouck, D. (2019). *Missing link: Africa and mathematics, culture, and the arts.* Springer International Publishing.

Hwang, S. (2020). Examining the effect of students' early numeracy activities at home on later mathematics achievement via early numeracy competencies and self-efficacy beliefs. *International Electronic Journal of Elementary Education, 13*(1), 47–56.

Jackson, S. A., & Marsh, H. W. (1996). Development and validation of a scale to measure optimal experience: The flow state scale. *Journal of Sport and Exercise Psychology, 18,* 17–35.

Jiménez, L., & Verschaffel, L. (2014). Development of children's solutions of nonstandard arithmetic word problem solving. *Infancia y Aprendizaje, 37*(3), 535–568.

Jones, B., & Lee, C. (2018). Fostering interpersonal relationships in diverse classrooms. *Educational Psychology Review, 30*(4), 589–604.

Joseph, G. G. (2000). *Crest of the peacock: Non-European roots of mathematics.* Princeton University Press.

Joseph, G. G. (1991). *The crest of the peacock: Non-European roots of mathematics.*

Kashdan, T. B., Rose, P., & Fincham, F. D. (2004). Curiosity and exploration: Facilitating positive subjective experiences and personal growth opportunities. *Journal of Personality Assessment. 82*(3), 291–305. https://doi.org/10.1207/s15327752jpa8203_05

Kant, D., & Sarikaya, D. (2020). Mathematizing as a virtuous practice: Different narratives and their consequences for mathematics education and society. *Synthese, 199*(1–2), 3405–3429.

Katz, V. J., & Imhausen, A. (Eds.). (2007). *The Mathematics of Egypt, Mesopotamia, China, India, and Islam: A sourcebook.* Princeton University Press.

Katz, V. J., & Imhausen, A. (2000). *Mathematics across cultures: The history of non-Western mathematics.*

Kaufman, A. S. (2009). *IQ testing 101.* Springer Publishing Company.

Kaufman, E., Lord, M., Reese, T., & Volkmann, J. (1949). The discrimination of visual number. *The American Journal of Psychology, 62,* 498–525.

Keat, J. B., & Wilburne, J. M. (2009). *The impact of storybooks on kindergarten children's mathematical achievement and approaches to learning. US-China Education Review, 6*(7), 61–67. ERIC. https://eric.ed.gov/?id=ED506319

Kilpatrick, J., Swafford, J., & Findell, B. (Eds.). (2001). *Adding it up: Helping children learn mathematics.* National Academy Press.

Klein, A. (2022). Ditch those math worksheets: The case for teaching real-world problem solving in K-5. *Education Week.* https://www.edweek.org/teaching-learning/ditch-those-math-worksheets-the-case-for-teaching-real-world-problem-solving-in-k-5/2022/05

Kliman, M. (2019, Fall). Storytelling math: Picture books as a vehicle for expanding views of math and who can do it. *Hands On! Magazine.*

Kogelman, S., & Warren, J. (1979). *Mind over math: Put yourself on the road to success by freeing yourself from math anxiety.* McGraw-Hill.

Kozol, J. (1991). *Savage inequalities: Children in America's schools.* Crown Publishers.

Kroeber, A. L., & Kluckhohn, C. (1952). *Culture: A critical review of concepts and definitions.* Vintage Books.

Lahey, J. (2014, January 21). Students should be tested more, not less. *The Atlantic.* https://www.theatlantic.com/education/archive/2014/01/students-should-be-tested-more-not-less/283195/

Lakatos, I. (1976) Proofs and refutations. *British Journal for the Philosophy of Science, 14.*

Larsen, N. E., Lee, K., & Ganea, P. A. (2018). Do storybooks with anthropomorphized animal characters promote prosocial behaviors in young children? *Developmental Science, 21*(3), e12590. https://doi.org/10.1111/desc.12590

Leap, W. L. (1988). Assumptions and strategies guiding mathematics problem solving by Ute students. In R. R. Cocking & J. P. Mestre (Eds.), *Cultural influences on learning mathematics* (pp. 161–186). Lawrence Erlbaum Associates.

Lehrer, R., & Schauble, L. (2003). Origins and evaluation of model-based reasoning in mathematics and science. In R. Lesh & H. M. Doerr (Eds.), *Beyond constructivism: Models and modeling perspectives on mathematics problem solving, learning, and teaching* (pp. 59–70). Lawrence Erlbaum.

Li, F. (2023) *The worlds I see.* Moment of Lift Books, Flatiron Books.

Livers, S. D., & Karp, K. S. (2018). The power of context: Promoting equity and access in mathematics learning using children's literature. In E. E. Monroe, T. A. Young, D. S. Fuentes, & O. H. Dial (Eds.), *Deepening students' mathematical understanding with children's literature* (pp. 130–168). National Council of Teachers of Mathematics.

Lumpkin, B. (1987). *African and African-American contributions to mathematics.* Portland Public Schools Geocultural Baseline Essay Series.

Luttenberger, S., Wimmer, S., & Paechter, M. (2018, August 8). Spotlight on math anxiety. *Psychological Research in Behavior Management, 11,* 311–322. https://doi.org/10.2147/PRBM.S141421

Merzbach, U., & Boyer, C. (2011). *A history of mathematics.* New Jersey.

Millmore, M. (2016). Newsletter 46. *Egyptian History Podcasts.* https://discoveringegypt.com/tag/egyptian-history-podcasts/

Montessori, M. (1912). *The Montessori method: Scientific pedagogy as applied to child education in "The Children's Houses" with additions and revisions by the author* (A. E. George, Trans.; H. W. Holmes, Introduction). Frederick A. Stokes Company.

NAEP. (2022). NAEP report card: 2022 NAEP Mathematics Assessment, https://www.nationsreportcard.gov/highlights/mathematics/2022/

National Council of Teachers of Mathematics. (1989). *Curriculum and evaluation standards for school mathematics.* Author.

National Council of Teachers of Mathematics. (2014). *Principles to actions: Ensuring mathematical success for all.* NCTM.

National Council of Teachers of Mathematics. (n.d.). Using identity and agency to frame access and equity. *Principles to Actions Toolkit.* https://www.nctm.org

/Conferences-and-Professional-Development/Principles-to-Actions-Toolkit/Using
-Identity-and-Agency-to-Frame-Access-and-Equity/

National Center for Education Statistics. (n.d.). Racial/ethnic enrollment in public schools (Indicator CGE). U.S. Department of Education. https://nces.ed.gov /programs/coe/indicator/cge/racial-ethnic-enrollment

Newmann, F. M., Secada, W. G., & Wehlage, G. G. (1995). *A guide to authentic instruction and assessment: Vision, standards, and scoring.* Wisconsin Center for Education Research.

Newmann, F. M., Wehlage, G. G., & Lamborn, S. D. (1992). The significance and sources of student engagement. In *Student engagement and achievement in American secondary schools* (pp. 11–39). Teachers College Press.

O'Connor, J. J., & Robertson, E. F. (2000). Mathematics in the Islamic world. http:// www-history.mcs.st-andrews.ac.uk/HistTopics/Islamic_mathematics.html

OECD. (2020). *Global teaching insights: A video study of teaching.* OECD Publishing. https://doi.org/10.1787/20d6f36b-en

Pekrun, R., & García, D. (2016). Math self-efficacy or anxiety? The role of emotional and motivational contribution in math performance. *Social Psychology of Education.*

Perrault, C. (1697). *Histoires ou contes du temps passé* [Tales of Mother Goose].

Peterson, L. (2017, November 14). The science behind the art of storytelling. Harvard Business Publishing. https://www.harvardbusiness.org/the-science-behind-the -art-of-storytelling/

Pinker, S. (2003). *How the mind works.* Penguin Books.

Polya, G. (1945). *How to solve it: A new aspect of mathematical method.* Princeton University Press.

Rauff, J. V. (1996). My brother does not have a pickup: Ethnomathematics and mathematics education. *Mathematics and Computer Education, 30*(1), 42–50. https://eric.ed .gov/?q=ethnomathematics&pg=6&id=EJ523602

Ritz, H. (2013). *Die Geschichte vom Rotkäppchen.* Kassel.

Robinson, D. et al. (2021). *Accelerating student learning with high-dosage tutoring.* EdResearch For Recovery. https://files.eric.ed.gov/fulltext/ED613847.pdf

Robinson, E. T. (2023). Count me in: Exploring equity, diversity, and inclusion through mathematics and children's literature. *The Reading Teacher, 77*(1), 3–14. https://doi .org/10.1002/trtr.2233

Romberg, T. A., Webb, D. C., Shafer, M. C., & Folgert, L. (2005). *Differences in performance between Mathematics in Context and conventional students* (Monograph No. 6). Wisconsin Center for Education Research, University of Wisconsin–Madison.

Roser, N., Martinez, M., Fuhrken, C., & McDonnold, K. (2007). Characters as guides to meaning. *The Reading Teacher, 60*(6), 548–559. http://www.jstor.org/stable /20204502

Roth, W.-M. (2003). Science education as/for participation in the community. *Science Education, 87*(2), 163–196.

Schein, E. H. (2010). *Organizational culture and leadership* (4th ed.). Jossey-Bass.

Schoenfeld, A. H. (1987). *Cognitive science and mathematics education.* Erlbaum.

Schoenfeld, A. H. (2002). How can we examine the connections between teachers' world views and their educational practices? *Issues in Education, 8*(2), 217–227.

Schoenfeld, A. H. (2014). Looking for leverage: Issues of classroom research on "Algebra for All." *Journal of Research in Mathematics Education, 45*(2), 219–235.

Shafer, M. C., Folgert, L., & Kwako, J. (2004). Opportunity to Learn with Understanding for 1998–1999 (Mathematics in Context Longitudinal/Cross-Sectional Study Technical Report No. 42). University of Wisconsin–Madison.

Shah, P. E., Weeks, H. M., Richards, B., & Kaciroti, N. (2018). Early childhood curiosity and kindergarten reading and math academic achievement. *Pediatric Research.* https://doi.org/10.1038/s41390-018-0039-3

Schultz, P. 1981. A very brief history of pure mathematics: The Ishango bone. University of Western Australia School of Mathematics. http://www.maths.uwa.edu.au/~schultz/3M3/history.html

Sipe, L. R. (1998). How picture books work: A semiotically framed theory of text-picture relationships. *Children's Literature in Education, 29*(2), 97–108.

Skemp, R. R. (1976). Relational understanding and instrumental understanding. *Mathematics Teaching, 77,* 20–26.

SLJ Staff. (2024, April 4). BIPOC representation in children's literature continues its slow rise, according to CCBC diversity statistics. *School Library Journal.* https://www.slj.com/story/BIPOC-Representation-Childrens-Literatures-Continues-Its-Slow-rise-According-CCBC-Diversity-Statistics

Smith, A. (2019). The role of intercultural learning in education. *Journal of Multicultural Education, 43*(2), 87–102.

Smith, D. (2024). Hidden figures: Giving history's most overlooked mathematicians their due. *The Guardian.* https://www.theguardian.com/books/article/2024/jul/29/secret-lives-numbers-history-mathematicians-overlooked

Smith, J. (2023, July 19). Ending California's math wars requires leadership from Sacramento. *EdSource.* https://edsource.org/2023/ending-californias-math-wars-requires-leadership-from-sacramento/684271

Spielberger, C. D. (1985). Anxiety, cognition and affect: A state-trait perspective. In A. H. Tuma & J. Maser (Eds.), *Anxiety and the anxiety disorders* (pp. 171–182). Lawrence Erlbaum Associates.

Tatar, M. (1999). *The classic fairy tales.* W.W. Norton & Company.

Thapa, A., Cohen, J., Guffey, S., & Higgins-D'Alessandro, A. (2013). A review of school climate research. *Review of Educational Research, 83*(3), 357–385.

Trakulphadetkrai, N. V., Aerila, J.-A., & Yrjänäinen, S. (2019). Bringing mathematics alive through stories. In K. J. Kerry-Moran & J.-A. Aerila (Eds.), *Story in children's lives: Contributions of the narrative mode to early childhood development, literacy, and learning* (pp. 191–206). Springer. https://doi.org/10.1007/978-3-030-19266-2_11

Treffers, A. (1978). *Wiskobas doelgericht.* IOWO.

Trezise, K., & Reeve, R. A. (2014, July 31). Cognition-emotion interactions: Patterns of change and implications for math problem solving. *Frontiers in Psychology, 5,* 840. https://doi.org/10.3389/fpsyg.2014.00840

UNESCO. (2013). *Intercultural competencies: Conceptual and operational framework.* United Nations Educational, Scientific and Cultural Organization.

Üzel, D. (2007). *The effect of realistic mathematics education (RME)–supported instruction on student achievement in 7th grade elementary mathematics education* (Unpublished doctoral dissertation). Balikesir University.

Valencia, R. R. (2010). *Dismantling contemporary deficit thinking: Educational thought and practice*. Routledge.

Verschaffel, L., Greer, B., & De Corte, E. (2002). Everyday knowledge and mathematical modeling of school word problems. In K. P. Gravemeijer, R. Lehrer, H. J. van Oers, & L. Verschaffel (Eds.), *Symbolizing, modeling and tool use in mathematics education* (pp. 171–195).

Volkov, A. (1998). Counting rods. In R. Bud and D. J. Warner (Eds.), *Instruments of science: A historical encyclopedia* (pp. 155–156). Garland.

Vygotsky, L. S. (1978). *Mind in society: The development of higher psychological processes*. Harvard University Press.

Weir, K. (2023, October 1). How to solve for math anxiety? Studying the causes, consequences, and prevention methods needed. *Monitor on Psychology, 54*(7), 44. https://www.apa.org/monitor/2023/10/preventing-math-anxiety

Weldon, L. G. (2023, January 23). *The way we teach math is all wrong*. Harvard Business Publishing.

Yglesias, M. (2018). The bell curve is about policy, and it's wrong. *Vox*. https://www.vox.com/2018/4/10/17182692/bell-curve-charles-murray-policy-wrong

Yuanita, P., Zulnaidi, H., & Zakaria, E. (2018, September 27). The effectiveness of Realistic Mathematics Education approach: The role of mathematical representation as mediator between mathematical belief and problem solving. *PLOS One, 13*(9), e0204847. https://doi.org/10.1371/journal.pone.0204847

Zipes, J. (1993). *The trials and tribulations of Little Red Riding Hood: Versions of the tale in sociocultural context*. Routledge.

Index

About the Authors

Gigi Carunungan, EdD, is an educational innovator reinventing learning environments that nurture students' potential. She co-founded and led the founding years of *Synapse School* and *Imagination School*, two progressive K–8 academies in Silicon Valley, where she designed learner-oriented integrated and thematic STEAM (science, technology, engineering, arts, and math) curricula, qualitative assessment, and teacher training programs.

Gigi developed the *Helical Model*™, a five-stage learning framework designed to cultivate children's higher-order thinking, problem-solving, and knowledge transfer. She also founded *Young Outliers*, a design-oriented K–12 summer camp that offers experiential programs like Design Math, Design Physics, and Design Entrepreneurship.

As Playnovate's Chief Learning Architect, Gigi led the learning design of over 300 online K–6 STEAM lessons. She is also the founder and CEO of MathXplorers, a company that publishes intercultural math stories, making math intuitive and engaging for all learners. In 2024, MathXplorers was selected for the Independent Book Publishers Association's Innovative Voices Program.

Gigi taught mathematics methods to teachers at San Jose State University and authored books titled *Digital Media in the Classroom* and *Documentary Moviemaking for Social Studies*. She holds a doctoral degree in Educational Leadership from San Jose State University and continues to innovate at the intersection of mathematics, storytelling, the arts, and entrepreneurship.

Jessica Liou is passionate about equitable access to quality education. She spent two years as a volunteer teacher at the Safe Passage School in Guatemala, teaching English and introducing advanced STEAM lessons to students from low-income backgrounds. This experience strengthened her commitment to creating affordable, engaging, and compelling learning opportunities for children worldwide.

MathXplorers marks Jessica's debut as an illustrator and book designer. She combines her artistic skills with her belief in non-traditional learning approaches. She encourages young learners to explore subjects that spark their curiosity inside and outside the classroom.

She is working towards a bachelor's degree in liberal arts with an emphasis on cognitive science. Outside of her studies, Jessica loves experimenting in the kitchen and spending time with her dog in her apartment in Queens.

Printed and bound by CPI Group (UK) Ltd, Croydon, CR0 4YY

17/06/2025

14690542-0002